THE LEADERSHIP CHALLENGE® WORKSHOP PARTICIPANT WORKBOOK

FOURTH EDITION

James M. Kouzes
& Barry Z. Posner

Pfeiffer
A Wiley Imprint
www.pfeiffer.com

Published by Pfeiffer
An Imprint of Wiley
989 Market Street
San Francisco, CA 94103-1741
www.pfeiffer.com

For additional copies/bulk purchases of this book in the U.S. please contact 800-274-4434.

Pfeiffer books and products are available through most bookstores. To contact Pfeiffer directly call our Customer Care Department within the U.S. at 800-274-4434, outside the U.S. at 317-572-3985, fax 317-572-4002, or visit www.pfeiffer.com.

Pfeiffer also publishes its books in a variety of electronic formats. Some content that appears in print may not be available in electronic books.

ISBN: 978-0-470-54355-9

Acquiring Editor: Lisa Shannon
Director of Development: Kathleen Dolan Davies
Development Editor: Janis Fisher Chan
Production Editor: Dawn Kilgore
Editor: Rebecca Taff
Manufacturing Supervisor: Becky Morgan
Design: izles design

Printed in the United States of America

Printing   10 9 8 7 6 5 4 3 2 1

CONTENTS

Welcome

LEADERSHIP IS EVERYONE'S BUSINESS

In today's world there are countless opportunities to make a difference. There are opportunities to restore hope and renew meaning in our lives. Opportunities to rebuild a sense of community and increase understanding among diverse peoples. Opportunities to turn information into knowledge and improve the collective standard of living. Opportunities to apply knowledge to products and services, creating extraordinary value for the customer. Opportunities to pursue peace when so many wage war. Opportunities to use the tools of technology to weave a web of human connection. Opportunities to find a better balance in our always–on, 24/7/365 lives. Opportunities to provide direction and support during uncertain times.

As there has been in all times of change and uncertainty, there is a need for people to seize these opportunities and lead us to greatness. There is a need for leaders to inspire us to dream, to participate, and to persevere. *The Leadership Challenge® Workshop* offers you the chance to do just that—to take the initiative, to seize the opportunities, and to make a difference.

Since 1982, when we began our research, we've been fortunate to hear and read the stories of thousands of ordinary men and women who have led others to get extraordinary things done. The stories we've collected are not from the famous politicians or corporate CEOs who so often get the credit. They're not from the media celebrities or legendary entrepreneurs.

The people we've studied are your neighbors, your colleagues, and your friends. People just like you. These choices are intentional. Without them—and you—nothing great would ever get done. And, if there's one singular lesson about leadership from all of the cases we've gathered it's this: **leadership is everyone's business**.

This is the truth that forms the foundation of *The Leadership Challenge® Workshop*. This is the truth that informs our selection of the stories we tell, the examples we give, and the activities we facilitate. We know that you can learn to become a better leader, and we know that you can make an even greater positive difference than you are now making.

Wanting to lead and believing that you can lead are the departure points on the path to leadership development. Stepping out there and exploring the territory, however, is the only way to learn, and that's how we've designed *The Leadership Challenge® Workshop*. It's a voyage of self-discovery that begins with an expedition into your inner terrain and ends with your commitment to guide others along the path to distinction.

Welcome aboard, and have fun!

JIM KOUZES & BARRY POSNER

● ● ● ● ● ● ● ● ● ● ● ● ● ● ● ●

❝Our strength as humans and as leaders has nothing to do with what we look like. Rather, it has everything to do with what we feel, what we think of ourselves.... Leadership is applicable to all facets of life.❞

VERONICA GUERRERO,
WINNING EDGE RESEARCH

ORIENTEERING

Managers vs. Leaders

MANAGER DEFINITION

man•ag•er [man-i-jer]

—noun

1. The root of the word manage is "manus," which means hand. Managers handle things—budgets, forecasts, schedules, etc. Their eyes are on today.

Related forms: man•ag•er•ship, noun

LEADER DEFINITION

lead•er [lee-der]

—noun

1. The root of the word lead is "to go, guide, or travel." It implies moving toward a new destination. A leader's eyes are on tomorrow as well as on today. So leading is about going somewhere—about guiding people on a journey.

Related forms: lead•er•less, adjective

Preparing for the Journey

We are all on our way to somewhere else. We are all making the journey into a changed world called "the future."

But we do not travel alone. We must work with others to make our dreams become realities. *The Leadership Challenge® Workshop* is about how leaders see, inspire, and achieve. It is also about how we can liberate the leader within each of us.

Join us on a journey along the leader's path. Join us as we explore how leaders get extraordinary things done in organizations.

This section is called Orienteering, after the sport that's been called "the thinking person's cross-country race." In orienteering, participants use a compass and a map to set the best and fastest course through unfamiliar territory.

Leadership is a lot like Orienteering. You're expected to find your way through the unknown and to help others find theirs. Just as there are no spectators in orienteering, there are no spectators in leadership. Everyone has an important role to play in charting the course to success.

Fundamentals

- Leadership is everyone's business.

- Leadership is a relationship.

- Leadership development is self-development.

- The best leaders are the best learners.

- Leadership development is not an event—it's an ongoing process.

- It takes practice—deliberate practice—to become a better leader.

- Leadership is an aspiration and a choice.

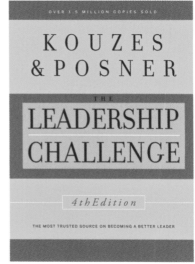

• • • • • • • • • •

66 **Leadership opportunities are presented to everyone.... What makes the difference between being a leader and not is how you respond in the moment.** 99

MICHELE GOINS,
CHIEF INFORMATION OFFICER FOR
HEWLETT-PACKARD'S IMAGING
AND PRINTING GROUP

What if someone walked into this room right now and said...

"Hi, I'm your new leader."

What are the questions you'd want to ask that person?

Who are you?
Where?
Why?
SWOT

Who are you?
Where are we headed?
What are you going to do?

Hint: See page 186

Workshop Objectives

As a result of participating in *The Leadership Challenge® Workshop*, you will be able to:

- Identify your leadership strengths and weaknesses.

- Clarify and communicate your fundamental values and beliefs.

- Set the example for others by aligning your actions with shared values.

- Express your image of the future.

- Inspire others to share a common vision.

- Search for opportunities to change and improve.

- Experiment with innovative ideas and learn from accompanying mistakes.

- Build collaboration, teamwork, and trust.

- Strengthen the ability of others to excel.

- Recognize the accomplishments of others.

- Apply the lessons learned in the workshop to a current organizational challenge.

My Objectives:

```
------------------------------------------------
................................................
------------------------------------------------
................................................
------------------------------------------------
```

ORIENTEERING MODULE OBJECTIVES

- Name and describe The Five Practices of Exemplary Leadership®.

- Use your *Leadership Practices Inventory* (LPI) feedback to identify the leadership behaviors in which you are strong and those in which you need to become more effective.

....

....

....

PLEASE: REFRAIN FROM USING YOUR CELL PHONE, COME BACK ON TIME FROM BREAKS, AND LISTEN WHEN OTHERS ARE SPEAKING.

Personal Best Leadership Experience

In preparing for this workshop, you wrote about your Personal Best as a leader. Take a few moments now to review your notes and get ready to tell your story. Be prepared to hear about some extraordinary accomplishments from your colleagues.

When you listen to your colleagues' stories, what behaviors, actions, and attitudes seem to be the keys to their leadership success?

Perserverance   (Commitment) or Never Give Up

What common leadership practices, actions, behaviors, or themes run through all the stories?

Consistency of values and commitment

The Five Practices of Exemplary Leadership®

How do you get other people to follow willingly, especially when you set out across unknown territory? How do you mobilize other people to move forward together in a common purpose? How do you get others to want to get extraordinary things done?

We interviewed more than five hundred individuals, reviewed more than twelve thousand case studies, and analyzed more than a million survey questionnaires to find out what leaders do to make themselves leaders when performing at their best.

By studying times when leaders performed at their personal best, we were able to identify Five Practices common to most extraordinary leadership achievements.

When leaders are at their best, they:

1. Model the Way

2. Inspire a Shared Vision

3. Challenge the Process

4. Enable Others to Act

5. Encourage the Heart

LEADERSHIP IS...

"THE ART OF mobilizing others TO want TO STRUGGLE FOR shared aspirations."

—JIM KOUZES AND BARRY POSNER

The Five Practices of Exemplary Leadership®

1. MODEL THE WAY

- Clarify values by finding your voice and affirming shared ideals.

- Set the example by aligning actions with shared values.

Walk the talk.   People follow our example even if you
tell them to do something else
        Credibility →   How do we model that?
        Professionalism.

2. INSPIRE A SHARED VISION

- Envision the future by imagining exciting and ennobling possibilities.

- Enlist others in a common vision by appealing to shared aspirations.

Toughest thing to do.

"The GM of a hotel must give a soul to the hotel"

You want to tell them this is where we want to go

If I don't manage to make you happy then you can't make our guests happy."

3. CHALLENGE THE PROCESS

- Search for opportunities by seizing the initiative and by looking outward for innovative ways to improve.

- Experiment and take risks by constantly generating small wins and learning from experience.

"You have to be consisten   You have to be persistent."

"We made a major change. That means the ground rules went out the window."

4. ENABLE OTHERS TO ACT

- Foster collaboration by building trust and facilitating relationships.

- Strengthen others by increasing self-determination and developing competence.

"If you don't know, you can't do better"

"It's not a job; it's a lifestyle."

"The Jedi mind trick" Let them "solve" the problem and come up with the solution that you are looking for.

5. ENCOURAGE THE HEART → Not sure at how well we do this.

- Recognize contributions by showing appreciation for individual excellence.

- Celebrate the values and victories by creating a spirit of community.

"At the store level, we celebrate our successes

The Leadership
Practices Inventory

- The LPI was developed to validate Jim Kouzes' and Barry Posner's findings from their Personal Best Leadership case studies. The research data consistently shows that leaders who engage in the behaviors measured by the LPI are more effective and successful than those who do not.

- The LPI has thirty behavioral statements, six for each of The Five Practices. You and your observers indicated how frequently you engaged in those behaviors on a scale ranging from 1, meaning "almost never" to 10, meaning "almost always."

- The LPI provides information about you and your observers' perceptions of your leadership behaviors; it does not evaluate your IQ, leadership style, management skill, or personality.

- Research demonstrates that increasing the frequency with which you engage in the behaviors measured by the LPI—in other words, The Five Practices—will make you a more effective leader.

For more about the research, visit www.leadershipchallenge.com/go/research.

What does the LPI measure?

What Do the Scores Mean?

Our research has shown that the higher your scores on the LPI-Observer, the more others perceive you as:

- Having a high degree of personal credibility

- Being effective in meeting job-related demands

- Being able to increase motivation levels

- Being successful in representing your group to upper management

- Having a high-performance team

- Fostering loyalty and commitment

- Reducing absenteeism and turnover and reducing stress levels

In addition, those working with you feel significantly more satisfied with your practices and strategies, more committed and more powerful and influential.

LPI
Leadership Practices Inventory

The Five Practices Data Summary

This page summarizes your LPI scores for each Practice. The Self column shows the total of your own responses to the six statements about each Practice. The AVG column shows the averages of all your Observers' ratings. The Individual Observers columns show the total of each Observer's rating. Scores can range from 6 to 60.

Manager **D**irect Report **C**o-Worker Other

AVG Average of all LPI Observer Ratings

	Self	AVG	M	D1	D2	D3	D4	C1	C2	O1	O2
Model the Way	45	46.0	40	49	50	32	50	51	45	50	47
Inspire a Shared Vision	39	40.6	50	38	36	31	48	39	39	44	40
Challenge the Process	41	45.7	49	48	49	26	51	47	49	46	46
Enable Others to Act	49	49.1	54	55	52	26	48	52	56	52	47
Encourage the Heart	44	45.1	48	54	49	23	48	47	38	47	52

ORIENTEERING | PAGE 19

Leadership Practices Inventory

The Five Practices Bar Graphs

These bar graphs, one set for each Practice, provide a graphic presentation of the numerical data recorded on The Five Practices Data Summary page. By Practice, it shows the total score for Self and the average total for each category of Observer. Scores can range from 6 to 60.

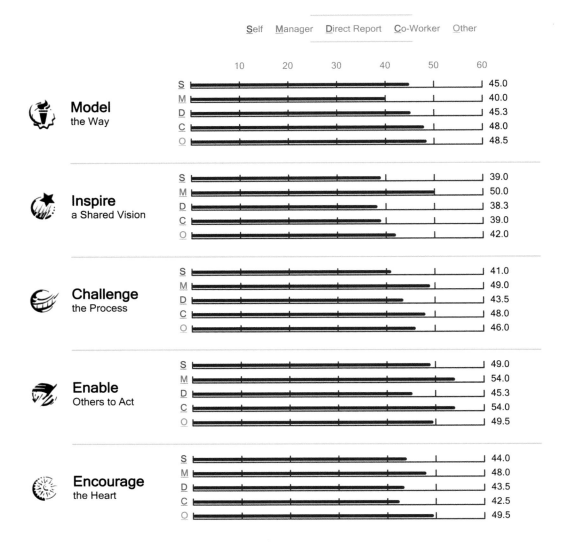

	Self	Manager	Direct Report	Co-Worker	Other

Model the Way

S	45.0
M	40.0
D	45.3
C	48.0
O	48.5

Inspire a Shared Vision

S	39.0
M	50.0
D	38.3
C	39.0
O	42.0

Challenge the Process

S	41.0
M	49.0
D	43.5
C	48.0
O	46.0

Enable Others to Act

S	49.0
M	54.0
D	45.3
C	54.0
O	49.5

Encourage the Heart

S	44.0
M	48.0
D	43.5
C	42.5
O	49.5

LPI
Leadership Practices Inventory

The rating scale runs from 1 to 10

1 - Almost Never	6 - Sometimes
2 - Rarely	7 - Fairly Often
3 - Seldom	8 - Usually
4 - Once in a While	9 - Very Frequently
5 - Occasionally	10 - Almost Always

Model the Way Data Summary
• Clarify values by finding your voice and affirming shared ideals
• Set the example by aligning actions with shared values

This page shows the scores for each of the six leadership behaviors related to this Practice. The Self column shows the scores you gave yourself for each behavior. The AVG column shows the averages of all the Observers' ratings. The Individual Observers columns show each Observer's rating for each behavioral item. Scores can range from 1 to 10.

Manager   **D**irect Report   **C**o-Worker   Other

AVG Average of all LPI Observer Ratings

		Self	AVG	M	D1	D2	D3	D4	C1	C2	O1	O2
1.	Sets a personal example of what is expected	8	8.0	9	8	10	4	8	8	8	9	8
6.	Makes certain that people adhere to agreed-on standards	7	7.8	6	9	9	6	7	10	9	8	6
11.	Follows through on promises and commitments	9	7.9	7	8	7	7	8	9	8	9	8
16.	Asks for feedback on how his/her actions affect people's performance	6	7.3	6	7	7	7	8	8	7	8	8
21.	Builds consensus around organization's values	8	7.3	6	8	10	3	9	7	7	8	8
26.	Is clear about his/her philosophy of leadership	7	7.7	6	9	7	5	10	9	6	8	9

ORIENTEERING | PAGE 21

LPI

Leadership Practices Inventory

The rating scale runs from 1 to 10

1 - Almost Never	6 - Sometimes
2 - Rarely	7 - Fairly Often
3 - Seldom	8 - Usually
4 - Once in a While	9 - Very Frequently
5 - Occasionally	10 - Almost Always

Model the Way Bar Graphs

- Clarify values by finding your voice and affirming shared ideals
- Set the example by aligning actions with shared values

The set of bar graphs for each of the six leadership behaviors related to this Practice provides a graphic representation of your and your Observers' average ratings for that behavior. Scores can range from 1 to 10.

Self   Manager   Direct Report   Co-Worker   Other

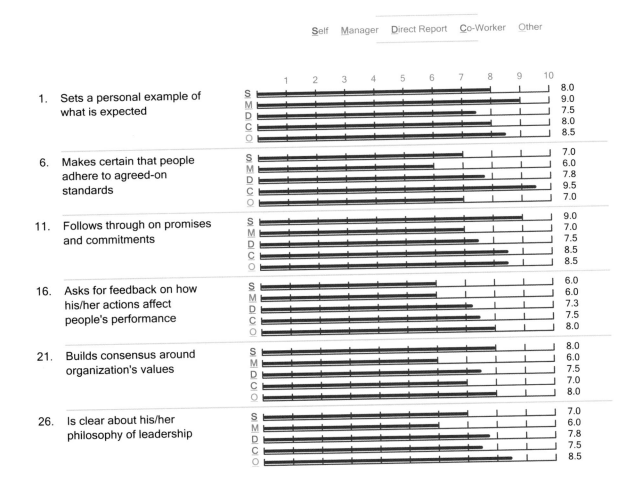

1.	Sets a personal example of what is expected	S M D C O	8.0 9.0 7.5 8.0 8.5
6.	Makes certain that people adhere to agreed-on standards	S M D C O	7.0 6.0 7.8 9.5 7.0
11.	Follows through on promises and commitments	S M D C O	9.0 7.0 7.5 8.5 8.5
16.	Asks for feedback on how his/her actions affect people's performance	S M D C O	6.0 6.0 7.3 7.5 8.0
21.	Builds consensus around organization's values	S M D C O	8.0 6.0 7.5 7.0 8.0
26.	Is clear about his/her philosophy of leadership	S M D C O	7.0 6.0 7.8 7.5 8.5

ORIENTEERING | PAGE 22

The rating scale runs from 1 to 10
1 - Almost Never   6 - Sometimes
2 - Rarely   7 - Fairly Often
3 - Seldom   8 - Usually
4 - Once in a While   9 - Very Frequently
5 - Occasionally   10 - Almost Always

Leadership Behaviors Ranking

This page shows the ranking, from most frequent ("high") to least frequent ("low") of all 30 leadership behaviors based on the average Observers' score. A horizontal line separates the 10 least frequent behaviors from the others. An asterisk (*) next to the Observer score indicates that the Observer score and the Self score differ by more than plus or minus 1.5.

High

		Practice	Self	Observer
14.	Treats others with dignity and respect	Enable	9	8.8
4.	Develops cooperative relationships	Enable	9	8.4
24.	Gives people choice about how to do their work	Enable	8	8.2
5.	Praises people for a job well done	Encourage	8	8.1
13.	Searches outside organization for innovative ways to improve	Challenge	6	8.1 *
1.	Sets a personal example of what is expected	Model	8	8.0
19.	Supports decisions other people make	Enable	8	8.0
28.	Experiments and takes risks	Challenge	7	8.0
11.	Follows through on promises and commitments	Model	9	7.9
3.	Seeks challenging opportunities to test skills	Challenge	8	7.9
9.	Actively listens to diverse points of view	Enable	8	7.9
30.	Gives team members appreciation and support	Encourage	8	7.8
6.	Makes certain that people adhere to agreed-on standards	Model	7	7.8
29.	Ensures that people grow in their jobs	Enable	7	7.8
26.	Is clear about his/her philosophy of leadership	Model	7	7.7
8.	Challenges people to try new approaches	Challenge	6	7.7 *
10.	Expresses confidence in people's abilities	Encourage	7	7.6
15.	Creatively rewards people for their contributions	Encourage	7	7.4
27.	Speaks with conviction about meaning of work	Inspire	7	7.4
21.	Builds consensus around organization's values	Model	8	7.3
22.	Paints "big picture" of group aspirations	Inspire	7	7.3
23.	Makes certain that goals, plans, and milestones are set	Challenge	7	7.3
16.	Asks for feedback on how his/her actions affect people's performance	Model	6	7.3
2.	Talks about future trends influencing our work	Inspire	7	7.1
20.	Recognizes people for commitment to shared values	Encourage	7	7.1
25.	Finds ways to celebrate accomplishments	Encourage	7	7.1
18.	Asks "What can we learn?"	Challenge	7	6.7
17.	Shows others how their interests can be realized	Inspire	6	6.3
7.	Describes a compelling image of the future	Inspire	6	6.2
12.	Appeals to others to share dream of the future	Inspire	6	6.1

Low

Difference between Observers' and Self rating was greater than 1.5

ORIENTEERING | PAGE 23

LPI

Leadership Practices Inventory

ORIENTEERING | PAGE **24**

Percentile Ranking

This page compares your Self scores and those of your Observers to the scores of several thousand people who have taken this version of the LPI. The horizontal lines at the 30th and 70th percentiles divide the graph into three segments, roughly approximating a normal distribution of scores.

S̲elf   M̲anager   D̲irect Report   C̲o-Worker   O̲ther

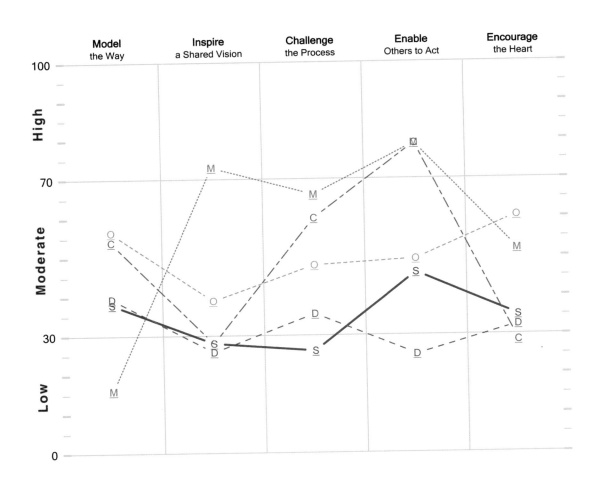

Reflecting on Your LPI Feedback

To keep in mind while reviewing your LPI report.

- There is no such thing as a "bad" or "good" score. The LPI scores are an objective, current view of your leadership behaviors—opportunities for you to become more comfortable and skillful as a leader.

- Look for messages in the data, not numbers. Ask "What are people trying to tell me about my leadership behaviors?"

- Take personal ownership of the scores. Remember that the purpose of is to identify what you can do to become a better leader.

- Avoid trying to figure out who D1 or C3 might be. Instead, concentrate on the messages.

- Do not be surprised if one observer rates you significantly lower in most if not all of the practices— that observer probably does not see you engaging in the practice behaviors very frequently.

Look through your report quickly. Use this space to note your initial reactions and first impressions.

1. What do you notice about the feedback? What surprises you? Pleases you?

Differences between the two Respondents

2. Does anything confuse you? Disappoint or upset you?

3. How does what you see in the feedback relate to what you learned from your and your colleagues' Personal Best stories?

4. Compare your self ratings with your observer ratings.

Practice with most agreement:

Practice with most disagreement:

Inspire A Shared vision

----

5. Compare your observers' responses with one another.

Practice with most agreement:

Practice with most disagreement:

----

6. How do you explain any inconsistencies between your ratings and those of the observers?

Between the ratings of the observers?

. . . .

. . . .

. . . .

List the six behaviors (the items numbered 1 to 30 on the Leadership Behaviors Ranking page) on which you rated yourself the highest, indicating that you engage in them most frequently.

Behavior:

_____

....

Practice:

_____

Behavior:

_____

....

Practice:

_____

Behavior:

_____

....

Practice:

_____

Behavior:

_____

....

Practice:

_____

Behavior:

....

Practice:

Behavior:

....

Practice:

Possible reasons?

....

....

List the six behaviors on which you rated yourself the lowest, indicating that you engage in them least often.

Behavior:

....

Practice:

Behavior:

....

Practice:

Behavior:

....

Practice:

Behavior:

....

Practice:

Behavior:

- -

. . . .

Practice:

- -

Behavior:

- -

. . . .

Practice:

- -

Possible reasons?

- -

. . . .

- -

. . . .

With your increased awareness about leadership, which six leadership behaviors would you like to be able to engage in more often?

Behavior number and name:

....

Action ideas:

....

Behavior number and name:

....

Action ideas:

....

Behavior number and name:

....

Action ideas:

....

Note any initial action ideas that occur to you for improving the frequency with which you engage in those behaviors.

Behavior number and name:

- -

. . . .

Action ideas:

- -

. . . .

Behavior number and name:

- -

. . . .

Action ideas:

- -

. . . .

Behavior number and name:

- -

. . . .

Action ideas:

- -

. . . .

What else did you notice about your feedback?

....

....

In which of The Five Practices are you the strongest? In which practice or practices could you use the most improvement?

Strongest:

....

Needs improvement:

....

What other thoughts, questions, or observations do you have about the messages from your LPI feedback?

....

....

Orienteering Summary

Think about where you are on your journey. If you were to leave the workshop now, what would you tell people back home is the most significant lesson you learned about yourself as a leader?

That sharing an inspired vision is a bigger area of opportunity than I had previously thought.

Modeling the way look close to my self evaluation with one and not with another person.

● ● ● ● ● ● ● ● ● ● ● ● ● ● ● ●

"If you want to lead others… you have to open up your heart… you have to be able to be honest with yourself in order to be honest with others. "

NEVZAT MERT TOPCU,
FOUNDER OF A MAGAZINE
ABOUT PC GAMES IN TURKEY

MODEL THE WAY

Clarify values by finding your voice and affirming shared ideals.

Set the example by aligning actions with shared values.

Model the Way

To model effectively, leaders must be clear about their guiding principles and then speak clearly and distinctly about what they believe. They also forge agreement about a set of common principles and ideas that make the organization unique and distinctive.

But eloquent speeches about personal values are not enough. Leaders stand up for their beliefs. They practice what they preach. They show others by their own example that they live by the values that they profess. Leaders know that, while their position may give them authority, it is their behavior that earns them the respect of their constituents. It is the consistency of word and deed that builds a leader's credibility.

MODULE OBJECTIVES

- Clarify and articulate the values that will guide your decisions and actions as a leader.

- Describe examples of how you can align your stated values with your everyday leadership behavior.

- Explain how you will lead your team to a consensus on shared values.

My Model the Way Feedback

SELF	OBSERVER AVERAGE	LEADERSHIP PRACTICES INVENTORY (LPI) ITEM
		**1**. I set a personal example of what I expect of others.
		**6**. I spend time and energy making certain that the people I work with adhere to the principles and standards we have agreed on.
		**11**. I follow through on the promises and commitments that I make.
		**16**. I ask for feedback on how my actions affect other people's performance.
		**21**. I build consensus around a common set of values for running our organization.
		**26**. I am clear about my philosophy of leadership.

Initial reactions:

Action ideas for getting better at this practice:

Characteristics of an Admired Leader

Percentage of Respondents Who Selected the Characteristic as One of the Seven Qualities They Most Admire in a Leader

THIS GROUP	% NORMS		THIS GROUP	NORMS	
1	*16*	**Ambitious** (aspiring, hardworking, striving)	➔ *4*	*89*	**Honest** ✗ Nat'l Top Pick (truthful, has integrity, trustworthy, has character, is trusting)
2	*35*	**Broad-minded** (open-minded, flexible, receptive, tolerant)	*1*	*17*	**Imaginative** (creative, innovative, curious)
1	*22*	**Caring** (appreciative, compassionate, concerned, loving, nurturing)	*0*	*4*	**Independent** (self-reliant, self-sufficient, self-confident)
3	*68*	**Competent** ✗ Nat'l Top Pick (capable, proficient, effective, gets the job done, professional)	➔ *5*	*69*	**Inspiring** ✗ Nat'l Top Pick (uplifting, enthusiastic, energetic, humorous, cheerful, positive about the future)
1	*25*	**Cooperative** (collaborative, team player, responsive)	*0*	*48*	**Intelligent** (bright, smart, thoughtful, intellectual, reflective, logical)
3	*25*	**Courageous** (bold, daring, fearless, gutsy)	➔ *4*	*18*	**Loyal** (faithful, dutiful, unswerving in allegiance, devoted)
2	*34*	**Dependable** (reliable, conscientious, responsible)	*1*	*15*	**Mature** (experienced, wise, has depth)
1	*25*	**Determined** (dedicated, resolute, persistent, purposeful)	*0*	*10*	**Self-controlled** (restrained, self-disciplined)
➔ *4*	*39*	**Fair-minded** (just, unprejudiced, objective, forgiving, willing to pardon others)	*3*	*36*	**Straightforward** (direct, candid, forthright)
➔ *4*	*71*	**Forward-looking** ✗ Nat'l Top Pick (visionary, foresighted, concerned about the future, sense of direction)	*2*	*35*	**Supportive** (helpful, offers assistance, comforting)

What Constituents Expect of Leaders

Four Characteristics of Admired Leaders

Competent

Forward-looking

Honest

Inspiring

The four characteristics that constituents expect of leaders add up to what communications experts refer to as **source credibility**. According to those experts, a source of information is considered believable when he or she is considered to possess the following three characteristics.

Components of Source Credibility

Experience / Expertise / Competence

Character / Trustworthy / Honesty

Dynamism → Inspiring

DWYSYWD

Do what you say you would do.

Research has shown that people consistently select four characteristics to describe the leaders they would choose to follow.

Impact of Credibility on an Organization

When people perceive their managers to have high credibility, they are more likely to:

- Be proud to tell others they're part of the organization.

- Feel a strong sense of team spirit.

- See their own personal values as consistent with those of the organization.

- Feel attached and committed to the organization.

- Have a sense of ownership of the organization.

When people perceive their managers to have low credibility, they're more likely to:

- Produce only if they're watched carefully.

- Be motivated primarily by money.

- Say good things about the organization publicly, but criticize it privately.

- Consider looking for another job in tough times.

- Feel unsupported and unappreciated.

How do leaders earn credibility? What is credibility behaviorally?

D___ W___ Y___ S___ Y___ W___ D___

Clarify Values

Values are the moral judgments, responses to others, and commitments to personal and organizational goals that:

- Help us determine what to do and what not to do.

- Influence every aspect of our lives.

- Set the parameters for our decisions we make every day.

Impact of Values Clarity on Commitment

Scale of 1 to 7

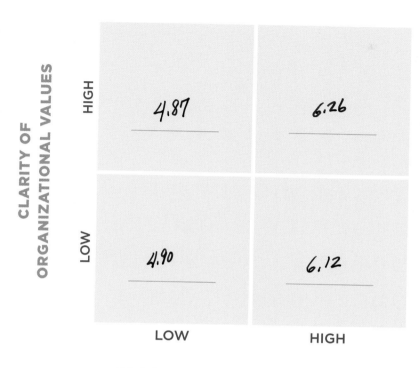

CLARITY OF ORGANIZATIONAL VALUES

HIGH

4.87

6.26

LOW

4.90

6.12

LOW

HIGH

CLARITY OF PERSONAL VALUES

● ● ● ● ● ● ● ● ● ● ●

❝ At the core of becoming a leader is the need to always connect one's voice to one's touch. ❞

MAX DE PREE,
FORMER CHAIRMAN AND CEO
OF HERMAN MILLER

Values Card Sort

Clarification of values begins with becoming more self-aware. This is an opportunity for you to sort out your personal values.

1. **Divide the Values Cards into three piles:**

- Values that are extremely important to you

- Values that are moderately important to you

- Values that are not important to you

2. **As you sort through the cards, think about the values that are most important to you.** Try to get the most important stack down to five values. Write those values in the five blank boxes on the next page.

3. **Discuss with your partner why you chose those five values—why they are so important to you.** If you are not clear about your partner's values, say, "I'm not yet clear on this value and why it's important to you. Please say more." Also, define the values that you chose—describe what each value means to you.

Defining Your Values

In the spaces below, record the top five values that you selected when you sorted the Values Cards. Briefly describe what each value means to you.

EXAMPLE

> **Creativity:** To be inventive and original

MY VALUE #1

Spirituality and Faith

MY VALUE #2

Family

MY VALUE #3

Patience

MY VALUE #4

Wisdom

MY VALUE #5

Truth

#6 Honesty / Integrity   #7 Harmony

Shared Values

The route to commitment begins by clarifying personal values. However, the greatest accomplishments are possible when the leader and the constituents share common values.

Shared values make a difference because they:

- Foster strong feelings of personal effectiveness.

- Promote high levels of company loyalty.

- Facilitate consensus about key organizational goals and stakeholders.

- Encourage ethical behavior.

- Promote strong norms about working hard and caring.

- Reduce levels of job stress and tension.

- Foster pride in the company.

- Facilitate understanding about job expectations.

- Foster teamwork and esprit de corps.

• • • • • • • • • • • • • • •

66 Understanding my values allows me to be more passionate about my work and gives a focus for what everyone on the team should be striving for. 99

JUAN GONZALES,
INDUSTRY SOLUTION MANAGER AT IBM

How One Leader Models the Way

What did this leader do and say to set the example?

VALUES/STANDARDS

**What the leader
SAYS is important**

Learn Something - Gift

P- Pi
R- Respect
I- Integrity
D- Diversity
E- empowerment

Went to the Frontline

Listened to concerns

ACTIONS

**What the Leader
Actually DOES**

Went to the frontline
Cross Trained Employees Got them
Raised.
Listened

• • • • • • • • • • • • • •

" My seeking feedback and listening in turn encourages my team to maintain open communication with other groups through enlisting their feedback and understanding the impact they can make to make their work more efficient. "

SEANG WEE,
CISCO SYSTEMS

Align Actions with Values

Here are some ways in which leaders demonstrate their values:

CALENDARS

How you choose to spend your time is the single clearest indicator of what's important to you. If you say something is important, then it had better show up on your calendar, on your meeting agendas, and in the places you go and people you see.

CRITICAL INCIDENTS

Chance occurrences and unexpected intrusions, which often occur during times of stress or change, bring into high relief questions of values. Critical incidents offer great opportunities to teach important lessons about appropriate norms of behavior.

STORIES

Stories are among the most important ways we pass along lessons from person to person, group to group, generation to generation. When someone says, "The moral of the story is…" you know he or she is about to communicate an important point. Leaders use stories to illustrate how values come to life in the organization. They can then serve as a kind of mental map that helps people know what is important and "how things are done around here."

LANGUAGE

Leaders choose their words carefully to make sure that people get the right message. They use metaphors—figures of speech in which a word or a phrase denoting one kind of idea is used in place of another—and analogies—words suggesting a resemblance in some ways between two things that are otherwise unlike—to enhance communication. And they ask questions to frame issues and set the agenda.

MEASUREMENTS

Measurement and feedback are essential to improved performance, so the outcomes and actions that are measured are the ones on which people focus. The LPI is also a measurement tool that helps you focus on a leader's critical behaviors.

REWARDS

The behaviors you reward, the people you recognize, and the accomplishments you celebrate send out signals about what matters to you. Make sure that, if you say a value is important, you tangibly and intangibly recognize performance that demonstrates the value.

Sample Values in Action Worksheet

CORE VALUE: CUSTOMER SERVICE

ACTION IDEAS

Calendar

- Answer customer services phones one morning per month.
- Visit client sites once a week.

Incidents

- The next time there is an unusual disruption in normal service, take on a frontline job to demonstrate that the customer comes first.
- Assign specific roles for staff members to take during service disruptions and have people practice these roles.

Stories

- Begin every staff meeting with customer stories, including both successes and learning opportunities.

Language

- Start referring to staff members as "associates" instead of as employees.
- Eliminate "subordinate" from your vocabulary. Eliminate "us/them" language from interdepartmental conversations.

Measurements

- Conduct a customer satisfaction survey.
- Determine the key leading indicators of your success and make them the key measures for the future.

Rewards

- Give a company-wide bonus for improving customer satisfaction rating.
- Set up an Applause! Bulletin Board for every location.

Values in Action Worksheet

CORE VALUE: _Family #2_

ACTION IDEAS

Calendar
- Make sure to schedule Allison & James time
- Make sure to schedule free time for Allison
- Make sure to schedule alone time with Allison

Incidents
- When a scheduling conflict arises practice saying "How can we work this out since I have time w/ Allison scheduled?"
-

Stories
-
-
-

Language
-
-
-

Measurements
-
-
-

Rewards
-
-

Commitment to Values To-Do List

☐ Schedule actions for modeling your values into your week.

☐ Set aside time in meetings to recognize people who are demonstrating a value.

☐ Ask people for feedback. Are you behaving consistently with your words?

☐ Weekly or monthly, do a quick values performance review at the end of financial and performance meetings.

Model the Way
Module Summary

Where are you on your journey to become a better leader?

> I think I have already begun the journey on becoming a better leader and there is much to learn. I am certainly willing and able therefore it will be an interesting journey.

Clarify values by finding your voice and affirming shared ideals.

Set the example by aligning actions with shared values.

What are the three most important things you learned about the practice of Model the Way?

1. How drastically people's views can be based on extenuating circumstances or a lack of interaction.

2. That I really need to keep my own true values in focus more and work through incidences that interupt themor conflict with them

3. It takes a lot of practice to get this to a point where others who don't interact with you may have a "proper perception" or view.

How will improving in the practice of Model the Way help you address the leadership challenge that you brought to this workshop?

Think about these questions.

How clear are you about the values and guiding principles that govern your decisions and actions in the context of this challenge? To what extent do others share those values and principles?

. . . .

. . . .

. . . .

. . . .

As you address this challenge, what are some things you can do to align your actions with your values so you will be seen as more credible?

. . . .

. . . .

. . . .

. . . .

Which of your key values might be "put to the test" as you work through this challenge? What support will you need to ensure that no values are compromised?

- -

. . . .

- -

. . . .

- -

. . . .

- -

. . . .

•••••••••••••••••

" I never asked anyone
to do anything I wouldn't
or couldn't do myself. "

MARY GODWIN,
RADIUS

● ● ● ● ● ● ● ● ● ● ● ● ● ● ● ●

" Never mistake a clear view for short distance. "

PAUL SAFFO

INSPIRE A SHARED VISION

Envision the future by imagining exciting and ennobling possibilities.

Enlist others in a common vision by appealing to shared aspirations.

Inspire a Shared Vision

There is no freeway to the future, no paved highway from here to tomorrow. There is only wilderness, uncertain terrain. There are no road maps, no signposts.

Like explorers, leaders have their skills and experience to prepare them. And while explorers rely on their compasses to determine direction, leaders steer by their dreams.

Leaders look forward to the future. They gaze across the horizon of time, imagining the opportunities that are in store once they and their constituents arrive at their destination. They have a sense of purpose and a desire to change the ways things are. Their clear vision of the future pulls them forward.

But leaders know that they cannot command commitment, only inspire it. They know that vision is a dialogue, not a monologue. They share their dreams so that others can understand and accept them. They learn about their team members' dreams, hopes, and aspirations and forge unity of purpose by showing them how the dream is for the common good. They communicate their passion through vivid language and expressive style.

MODULE OBJECTIVES

- Describe your vision for the future of your organization that appeals to higher-order values.

- Engage others in conversation about your vision of the future for your organization.

- Show team members how their long-term interests can be realized by enlisting in a common vision.

My Inspire a Shared Vision Feedback

SELF	OBSERVER AVERAGE			LEADERSHIP PRACTICES INVENTORY (LPI) ITEM
8	4	8	6	**2.** I talk about future trends that will influence how our work gets done.
8	3	3	3	*__**7.** I describe a compelling image of what our future could be like.
6	1	8	4.5	*__**12.** I appeal to others to share an exciting dream of the future.
6	7	7	7	**17.** I show others how their long-term interests can be realized by enlisting in a common vision.
9	4	9	6.5	**22.** I paint the "big picture" of what we aspire to accomplish.
8	2	9	5.5	*__**27.** I speak with genuine conviction about the higher meaning and purpose of our work.

Initial reactions:

....

....

....

....

Action ideas for getting better at this practice:

....

....

....

....

....

Definition of a Vision

A vision pulls people forward. It projects a clear image of a possible future. It generates the enthusiasm and energy to strive toward the goal.

IDEAL (a high standard to aspire to)

Visions are about hopes, dreams, and aspirations. They're about making a difference. They tell us the ennobling purpose and greater good we are seeking.

UNIQUE (pride in being different, an identity)

Visions are about the extraordinary. They are about what makes us distinctive, singular, and unequaled.

IMAGE (a concept or mental picture made real or tangible through descriptive language)

Word pictures, metaphors, examples, stories, symbols, and similar communication methods all help make visions memorable.

FUTURE-ORIENTED (looking toward a destination)

Visions describe an exciting possibility for the future. They stretch our minds out into the future and ask us to dream.

COMMON GOOD (a way people can come together)

Visions are about developing a shared sense of destiny. Leaders must be able to show others how their interests are served and how they are a part of the vision in order to enlist others in it.

A vision is an **IDEAL** and **UNIQUE IMAGE** of the **FUTURE** for the **COMMON GOOD.**

I Have a Dream

DELIVERY/LANGUAGE

THEMES

INSPIRING OTHERS

66 In the stream of time, the future is always with us. The directions and turns the world will take are embedded in the past and in the present. We often recognize them retrospectively, but our purpose is to anticipate what lies ahead. 99

JOHN NAISBITT,
AUTHOR OF *MEGATRENDS*

Envision the Ideal and Unique Future

Use these questions as a guide for describing your vision of an ideal and unique future.

Are you in your job to do something or for something to do?

To do something: To support and service the BSA mission

What about what your job is important to you, your team, your organization, to those who use your product or service?

That we teach young people values character development and how to make ethical choices and decisions over their lifetimes.

What would give your work real meaning and purpose—inspire you to come to work every day full of energy and enthusiasm?

That message was more fully understood by the volunteers and they would keep that in focus.

What legacy would you aspire to leave when it's time to move to a new opportunity?

That the volunteers understand
that the BSA mission is A legacy
to give other generations as well
as those as we are helping now.

What is your vision theme?

BSA mission
Continuing it in the future

• • • • • • • • • • • • • •

66 **One of the greatest gifts you can give others is the understanding that they can think bigger things than they believe they can. It's contagious. What limits vision in an organization is nobody being willing to speak up for one. But once you do, there is a sort of avalanche or landslide factor; it just keeps rolling. 99**

DAN SCHWAB
FORMER DIRECTOR OF
TRAINING AND DEVELOPMENT,
THE TRUST FOR PUBLIC LAND

Create Memorable Images

To *Inspire a Shared Vision* you have to create memorable images in other people's minds.

PARIS?

Images come forward when one thinks about this word.

TUVA?

T
World renown for a way of singing in the throat.

Breathe Life into Your Vision of the Future

Draw a "mind map" to illustrate one of your themes.

1. Select one of the themes you identified in the previous activity (page 79).

2. Write your theme in the circle in the middle of the page.

3. Illustrate your theme with word pictures by making all the associations you can with that theme—things, sounds, images, feelings, people, places—anything that comes to mind.

Finace and the future of BSA

New Tiger Cubs

Financial
Solvency
New Leaders

Funding for all

No Bills
Motivated
Leaders

Debt
Free

New Programs
Exciting
Daring

A
Legacy:
The
BSA
Mission

Property
Development
Improvement

No Child
left inside

Renovations

Healthy
Successful
Families

Endowment

No Bullying
Cool Scouting

Clarifying Your Vision of the Future

Review the notes you have made in this section. Then use the questions below to select the distinctive qualities of your vision—qualities that will move others.

IDEAL

What is your ideal work community? In what do you absolutely believe or feel passionately about? What is your dream about your work? Describe the perfect realization of your vision.

....

....

....

UNIQUE

What qualities make the future of your organization (or department, plant, project, etc.) distinctive, one of a kind? What would make it stand out and be different from everything else? What would make people proud? What distinctive legacy would you like to leave behind?

- -
. . . .
- -
. . . .
- -
. . . .

IMAGE

What is your vision like? What symbol, metaphor or simile, image, example, or mental picture most vividly represents your ideal and unique future?

- -
. . . .
- -
. . . .
- -

FUTURE-ORIENTED

To make sure your ideal and unique image is for the long term, ask yourself, "What are the trends that are propelling my vision?" As you look out five to ten years, what developments and changes do you see in your industry, your employees, your organizational partners, and your customers or clients?

- -

. . . .

- -

. . . .

- -

. . . .

COMMON GOOD

Who are your key constituents? What values and goals do they share? What does your vision offer them? How will you need to shape your vision so that it appeals to all your key constituents?

- -

. . . .

- -

. . . .

- -

. . . .

Inspire a Shared Vision Module Summary

Envision the future by imagining exciting and ennobling possibilities.

Enlist others in a common vision by appealing to shared aspirations.

What are the three most important things you learned about the practice of Inspire a Shared Vision?

1. ....
   -
   ....

2. ....
   -
   ....

3. ....
   -
   ....

How will improving in the practice of Inspire a Shared Vision help you address the leadership challenge that you brought to this workshop?

Think about these questions.

How clear are you about the important themes and the higher-order values that give your life and work meaning and direction? About those of your constituents?

What themes, hopes, dreams, and aspirations do you think that you share with your constituents and your organization?

In what ways can clarifying your vision of the future and enlisting others in a common vision help you address this leadership challenge?

....

....

....

....

Ideas into Action

• • • • • • • • • • • • •

66 I believed. Believing is a very important part of the action. You have to have faith. If you don't have that, then you're lost even before you get started. **99**

LAILA RAZOUK,
DEVELOPMENT TEAM MANAGER
FOR THE PCNET DIVISION OF
ADVANCED MICRO DEVICES

● ● ● ● ● ● ● ● ● ● ● ● ● ● ●

"Sometimes you just can't predict where the change will come from, but you have to have your eyes wide open if you have any hope of even catching a glimpse of it.**"**

MICHAEL PRIEST,
CEO OF BAY AREA CREDIT SERVICES

CHALLENGE
THE PROCESS

Search for opportunities by seizing the initiative and by looking outward for innovative ways to improve.

Experiment and take risks by constantly generating small wins and learning from experience.

Challenge the Process

Movie: Apollo 13

Challenge is the opportunity for greatness. Leaders welcome opportunities to test their abilities. They look for innovative ways to improve their work and their organization.

Leaders venture out. They are willing to step in to the unknown. They know that innovation comes more from listening than from telling. They seek and recognize good ideas and challenge the system to get those ideas adopted.

Great leaders are great learners. They know that risk taking involves mistakes and failure, so they treat the inevitable disappointments as learning opportunities. They are willing to experiment and take risks in order to find new and better ways of doing things. Leaders also create safe environments in which others can learn from their failures as well as their successes.

MODULE OBJECTIVES

- In the context of shared vision and values, look for new ideas outside the boundaries of the organization.

- Take incremental steps in applying new and innovative solutions.

- Create a climate in which people are willing to take risks and learn from mistakes.

One Leader Who Took the Challenge

CHALLENGE THE PROCESS | PAGE 96

My Challenge the Process Feedback

SELF	OBSERVER AVERAGE	LEADERSHIP PRACTICES INVENTORY (LPI) ITEM
7	2 8 5	**3**. I seek out challenging opportunities that test my own skills and abilities.
9	5 8 6.5	**8**. I challenge people to try out new and innovative ways to do their work.
7	3 7 5	**13**. I search outside the formal boundaries of my organization for innovative ways to improve what we do.
8	4 8 6	**18**. I ask "What can we learn?" when things don't go as expected.
8	6 8 7	**23**. I make certain that we set achievable goals, make concrete plans, and establish measurable milestones for the projects and programs that we work on.
8	2 5 3.5	**28**. I experiment and take risks, even when there is a chance of failure.

Initial reactions:

· ·

· ·

· ·

· ·

Action ideas for getting better at this practice:

· ·

· ·

· ·

· ·

· ·

Don't Forget

People are often **at their best** when dealing with significant change, difficulties, problems, adversity, and other challenges.

Getting extraordinary things done is often about small wins or "**little victories**."

No one gets it perfect the first time they try something new. **The best leaders are the best learners—** and the best creators of a learning environment.

• • • • • • • • •

❝ A desk is a dangerous place from which to watch the world. ❞

JOHN LE CARRÉ

Outsight

Where do good ideas come from? What are some ways you can use outsight—to search for opportunities and innovative ideas outside your team, organization, or industry?

- -
. . . .
- -
. . . .
. . . .
- -
. . . .
- -
. . . .
- -
. . . .
- -

Get out of the box.

Take Risks and Learn from Mistakes

#1. You have to keep working on trust and never take it for granted.

#2. Sometimes trust breaks down. When it does, see Rule #1.

. . . .

. . . .

. . . .

. . . .

. . . .

Rules for building and maintaining a climate of trust

Helping People Take Risks and Learn from Mistakes

What generalizations would you make about making mistakes and creating a learning environment?

....

....

....

How can you create an environment in which people learn from the inevitable mistakes of doing something new?

....

....

....

Hint: See page 186

66 When my employees make mistakes trying to improve something, I give them a round of applause. No mistakes means no new products. If they ever become afraid to make one, my company is doomed. 99

JIM READ,
PRESIDENT, THE READ CORPORATION

One Hop at a Time

What are all the little things that the leader did to make progress?

Small Wins

Small wins create a pattern of winning that attracts people who want to be allied with a successful venture.

Leaders identify the place to get started and begin by modeling action. Breaking big, even overwhelming problems into small, manageable chunks is an important aspect of creating small wins. Leaders work hard at finding ways to make it easy for the team to succeed.

What makes small wins so successful in creating momentum for change?

....

....

....

....

....

Why use small wins?

● ● ● ● ● ● ● ● ● ● ● ● ●

❝ You do big things by doing lots of small things. ❞

PHILIP DIEHL,
DIRECTOR OF THE U.S. MINT

Take It One Step at a Time

CURRENT CHALLENGE	OBSTACLE(S)	SMALL-WIN OPPORTUNITIES
Need additional Volunteer leadership at the district and unit levels (Add depth @ district cmte)	Other volunteers say "We can't find anyone Recruit anyone It's always the same people doing everything	Recruit 1 new person for Dist. cmte. each Month. Establish Tiger Fun Day for Unit leaders

Key Actions for Generating Small Wins

- Break it down. Break big problems down into small, doable pieces.

- Make a model. Create a small-scale version of what you're trying to do so you can see whether it will work.

- Keep it simple. Your visions should be grand, but keep your actions as simple as possible.

- Do the easy parts first. Help the group discover that they can do it.

- Accumulate YESES. Ask for agreement to do the first thing, then the second, then the third, etc.

- Experiment. Try, fail, learn, then try again.

- Give feedback. Let people know how they are doing.

- Celebrate. When you reach milestones, take the time to congratulate one another.

Challenge the Process
Module Summary

Leadership is closely associated with change and innovation.

Leaders actively seek and create new opportunities. They're always looking for new ideas within the context of their values and vision.

Leaders are willing to experiment and take risks. They see mistakes as opportunities to learn, and they create a climate in their organizations in which others can generate small wins and learn from their mistakes.

What are the three most important things you learned about the practice of Challenge the Process?

1. ....
....
....

2. ....
....
....

3. ....
....
....

Search for opportunities by seizing the initiative and by looking outward for innovative ways to improve.

Experiment and take risks by constantly generating small wins and learning from experience.

How will improving in the practice of Challenge the Process help you address the leadership challenge that you brought to this workshop?

Think about these questions.

Where can you look for creative, innovative ideas for addressing this challenge?

....

....

....

What can you do to take this challenge one step at a time so you can generate small wins?

....

....

....

....

Is it time for an experiment or a risk? What is that next step, and how can you support yourself in taking it?

. . . .

. . . .

. . . .

. . . .

. . . .

. . . .

. . . .

Ideas into Action

• • • • • • • • • • • • • • •

66 **The real dividing line is passion. As long as you believe what you're doing is meaningful, you can cut through fear and exhaustion and take the next step.** 99

ARLENE BLUM,
PH.D. IN BIOPHYSICAL CHEMISTRY,
AVID MOUNTAIN CLIMBER

● ● ● ● ● ● ● ● ● ● ● ● ● ● ● ● ●

"The best way for me to give power to other people… is to allow creativity and freedom to explore new ideas and ways of thinking."

JILL CLEVELAND,
FINANCE MANAGER OF APPLE, INC.

PRACTICE 4

ENABLE OTHERS TO ACT

Foster collaboration by building trust and facilitating relationships.

Strengthen others by increasing self-determination and developing competence.

Enable Others to Act

Leaders don't travel alone. Leaders know that the team effort to make grand dreams become reality requires solid trust and strong relationships. Leaders foster collaboration. They nurture self-esteem in others and make them feel strong and capable. Leaders make sure that when they win, everybody wins.

Leaders make it possible for others to do good work. They build teams with spirit, cohesion, and a true sense of community. Leaders involve others in making plans and decisions, and develop collaborative goals and cooperative relationships.

Leaders strengthen and develop others by sharing power and information, and by giving others visibility and credit. As coaches and teachers, they give people challenging tasks, support them with the tools they need to be successful, and clear obstacles from their paths.

MODULE OBJECTIVES

- Identify the actions leaders take that make people feel powerful and those that make them feel powerless.

- Describe several actions you can take to strengthen others in your organization.

- Describe actions that hinder and actions that facilitate building trust and collaboration in your organization.

My Enable Others to Act Feedback

SELF	OBSERVER AVERAGE	LEADERSHIP PRACTICES INVENTORY (LPI) ITEM
8	3 7 5	**4**. I develop cooperative relationships among the people I work with.
9	7 7 7	**9**. I actively listen to diverse points of view.
9	3 8 5.5	**14**. I treat others with dignity and respect.
9	5 3 3	**19**. I support the decisions that people make on their own.
9	3 3 3 3.	**24**. I give people a great deal of freedom and choice in deciding how to do their work.
8	6 7 6.5	**29**. I ensure that people grow in their jobs by learning new skills and developing themselves.

Initial reactions:

_____

....

_____

....

_____

....

_____

Action ideas for getting better at this practice:

_____

....

_____

....

_____

....

_____

....

_____

Powerful Times, Powerless Times

Think of a time or times when you felt **powerful** as a result of what someone said or did.

Describe what the person said and/or did. Be as specific as you can.

Ron Green - Scout Executive promoted me and stated that the Scout Reach Program had been abandoned & he ^{but} wanted me to take it over and develop it into a successful Scouting program. He said he believed I could do it.

Think of a time or times when you felt **powerless** as a result of what someone said or did.

Describe what the person said and/or did. Be as specific as you can.

What is the impact on your productivity and your morale when someone does or says something that makes you feel powerful?

Do you empower them?

. . . .

. . . .

What is the impact on your productivity and your morale when someone does or says something that makes you feel powerless?

Michael
Abarshoff

" It's your ship."

. . . .

. . . .

What are the implications for you as a leader?
Share your reasoning.

. . . .

. . . .

. . . .

Powerful Times

- Behaviors that make people feel powerful are enabling, and those that make people feel powerless are disabling.

- Feeling powerful is likely to bring out the best, most positive, most committed energy and performance.

- Making people feel capable and valued is at the heart of trust—the essential ingredient in people's willingness to take risks that can drive extraordinary results.

What have you said or done recently to enable your constituents by making them feel powerful?

Cite examples and be as specific as you can. Describe WHEN you actually did or said WHAT to enable WHOM.

- -

. . . .

- -

. . . .

- -

Movies like
Hoosiers

The Miracle Worker
"Annie Sullivan"

What have you said or done recently that might have been disabling to your constituents and made them feel powerless? Be specific.

- -

. . . .

- -

. . . .

- -

What barriers get in the way of enabling others?

What could you do to remove or reduce these barriers?

- -

. . . .

- -

. . . .

- -

How One Leader Strengthens Others

LEADER'S ACTIONS

LEADER'S CONTRIBUTIONS

LEADER'S RELATIONSHIPS

WHAT CAN YOU DO?

How to Give People More Control of Their Work

Thinking about what a leader can say or do to Enable Others to Act, what advice would you give a new leader on how to give people more control of their work?

....

....

....

....

....

....

....

....

Hint: See page 187

Developing Competence

We feel more capable and confident when we have the ability to perform well, and others have more confidence in us when they know we are competent. Leaders know that people need coaching to increase their competence and that, unless people have opportunities to put their talents to use, they'll end up bored or frustrated.

Think about the relationship that three or four of your team members have to the work they do. Write their initials or code names in the appropriate places on the flow chart.

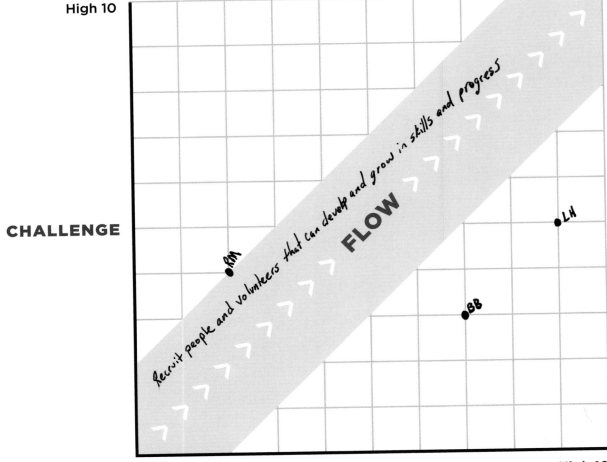

Why did you place each person's initials in those specific places on the flow chart?

What could you do to move that team member into or closer to the "flow"?

Name/Initials:

BB

Action:

Recruiting more Cmsrs to do cmsr Role

Name/Initials:

LH

Action:

Recruit More District People

Name/Initials:

RM

Action:

Recruit FOS Presenters
& Boy Scouters for Finane

Name/Initials:

Action:

Source: Based on the work of M. Csikszentmihalyi

• • • • • • • • • • • • • • •

66 **We helped everyone become more competent by creating a learning climate where people looked beyond their own job descriptions and organizational boundaries.** 99

RAJ LIMAYE,
DEPUTY MANAGER OF DATAPRO

• • • • • • • • • • •

66 I understood that in order for my employees, and thus myself, to be successful I needed to learn to develop a cohesive and collaborative team, beginning with trust as the framework. 99

JILL CLEVELAND,

FINANCE MANAGER OF APPLE, INC.

Experiencing Collaboration

Based on what you learned from the experiential activity, what advice would you give a leader who wants to foster collaboration in his or her organization? Be as specific as possible.

• • • • • • • • • • •

66 The best, most efficient, most profitable way to operate a business is to give everybody in the company a voice in saying how the company is run and a stake in the financial outcome, good or bad. 99

JACK STACK,

CEO OF SRC HOLDINGS

Building Trust

Think of a person or group with whom you want to increase trust. What can you do and say to build that trust?

....

....

....

....

....

....

....

Develop Cooperative Goals and Roles

Shared goals and shared roles bind people together in collaborative pursuits. As individuals work together and recognize that they need each other in order to be successful, they become convinced that everyone should contribute and that, by cooperating, they can accomplish the task successfully.

Leaders should think about what they can do to **foster collaboration in a given situation**—how they can structure the situation so that each member of the team must contribute to the success and so that no one wins unless everyone wins.

Enable Others to Act Module Summary

Foster collaboration by building trust and facilitating relationships.

Strengthen others by increasing self-determination and developing competence.

"You can't do it alone" is a mantra of the most exemplary leaders. You simply can't get extraordinary things done by yourself. Leaders know that collaboration is the master skill that enables teams, partnerships, and other alliances to function effectively.

Leaders also know that teams can't function without strong individuals. Strengthening others is essentially the process of making people feel capable of acting on their own initiative. Exemplary leaders use their power in service of others because they know that capable and confident people perform better.

What are the three most important things you learned about the practice of Enable Others to Act?

1. ....

....

2. ....

....

3. ....

....

How **will improving in the practice of Enable Others to Act help you address the leadership challenge that you brought to this workshop?**

Think about these questions.

How close are you to being in the flow vis-à-vis this challenge? Write your initials in the appropriate place on the flow chart to the right.

. . . .

. . . .

. . . .

What's the relationship between the level of the challenge and the level of your competencies and skills? How do you feel about that? What can you do to move yourself closer to the flow?

. . . .

. . . .

. . . .

. . . .

. . . .

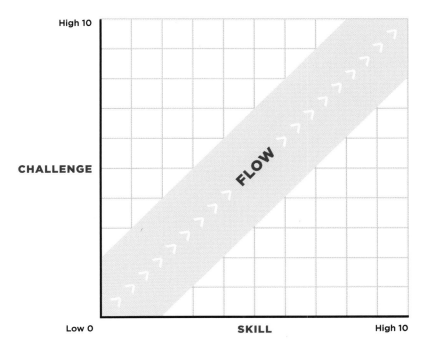

High 10

CHALLENGE

FLOW

Low 0

SKILL

High 10

To address this challenge, do you need to increase your team members' abilities to act? If so, what actions can you take to do that?

- -

. . . .

- -

. . . .

- -

. . . .

- -

. . . .

Ideas into Action

● ● ● ● ● ● ● ● ● ● ● ● ●

" [As a leader] you never assume control of the issue. They [employees] own it, not you. You coach and you mentor, but you make them decide and act. If it's their plan, they're more likely to make it happen. I helped add what I consider the most important ingredient: mutual respect and a feeling of togetherness. "

BRIAN BAKER
FAMILY-PRACTICE PHYSICIAN
AND COLONEL IN U.S. ARMY

" A sincere word of thanks from the right person at the right time can mean more to an employee than a raise, a formal award, or a whole wall of certificates and plaques. "

BOB NELSON,
1001 WAYS TO REWARD EMPLOYEES

ENCOURAGE THE HEART

Recognize contributions by showing appreciation for individual excellence.

Celebrate the values and victories by creating a spirit of community.

Encourage the Heart

Getting extraordinary things done in organizations is hard work. People become exhausted, frustrated, and disenchanted. Leaders Encourage the Heart of their team members to carry on. They inspire others with courage and hope.

To keep hope and determination alive, leaders show genuine appreciation for individual excellence. They express pride in the accomplishments of their team, and they make everyone feel like everyday heroes.

MODULE OBJECTIVES

- Give examples of meaningful recognitions.

- Identify actions you can take to Encourage the Heart of your team members.

My Encourage the Heart Feedback

SELF	OBSERVER AVERAGE			LEADERSHIP PRACTICES INVENTORY (LPI) ITEM
9	6	8	7	**5**. I praise people for a job well done.
8	5	2	3.5	**10**. I make it a point to let people know about my confidence in their abilities.
8	6	9	7.5	**15**. I make sure that people are creatively rewarded for their contributions to the success of our projects.
8	5	3	4	**20**. I publicly recognize people who exemplify commitment to shared values.
9	5	3	4	**25**. I find ways to celebrate accomplishments.
9	5	8	6.5	**30**. I give members of the team lots of appreciation and support for their contributions.

Initial reactions:

Action ideas for getting better at this practice:

Most Meaningful Recognition Activity

Think about one of the most meaningful recognitions you have ever received. It can be related to any part of your life—work, family, school, or community. What was the recognition? Why did you receive it? What made it so meaningful for you? Be as specific as you can.

Shofar Award - I was the Staff Advisor to the

CNJC JCoS. I assisted them in doing several things

over 3 plus years and they awarded me the Shofar

Award at their Annual Award Banquet. Not being
Jewish it was indeed humbling also due to the fact
that it had to be approved by the Scout Executive
Being the Guest speaker at my old districts (1st Assignment)
Volunteer Recognition Dinner.

What are some of the common elements that you heard from your colleagues' most meaningful recognition stories?

Appreciated

Positive to Negative Ratio

PNR

Research shows that people who engage in 3:1 at least three positive interactions for every negative interaction tend to be more effective and productive than those who have a lower ratio of positive to negative interactions.

FROM *HOW FULL IS YOUR BUCKET*, BY TOM RATH AND DONALD CLIFTON

The Essentials of Encourage the Heart

EXPECT THE BEST

Successful leaders have high expectations of themselves and of others. People frequently step up to higher levels of performance when expectations are high. Leaders bring out the best in others by making sure that people know what is expected of them and by encouraging them to be their best.

PERSONALIZE RECOGNITION

Leaders pay attention to remarkable achievements as well as achievements that are relatively small in scope, yet are personal breakthroughs, and recognize them. A cornerstone of meaningful recognition is that it is perceived as personal. For example, leaders tell stories with vivid details that reinforce **why** a person is being recognized. Personalized recognition lets people know they are valued as unique individuals and that their leaders have a thoughtful and personal interest in their accomplishments.

CREATE A SPIRIT OF COMMUNITY

Leaders not only recognize individual excellence, but they celebrate team values and victories. Celebrating together creates a heightened sense of community, belonging, and inclusion. It sends a message that everyone benefits when great things occur and reminds people of the enormous potential of what can be accomplished together.

BE PERSONALLY INVOLVED

You cannot delegate affairs of the heart. As a leader you must search for examples of people doing things right. You must be willing to look people in the eye and tell them thank you. You must be personally involved with people, so you know when they are worthy of special recognition or need reassurance or guidance when they have tough work to do. Your acts of encouragement send very clear messages about the importance and legitimacy of what people do.

● ● ● ● ● ● ● ● ● ● ● ● ●

" If everyone is doing a great job, what's the problem in letting them know that? "

LINDSAY LEVIN,
WHITES GROUP CHAIRMAN

Movies
:"Rudy"

How One Leader
Encourages the Heart

Keeping the four essentials in mind, pay close attention to
what the leader **does**.

**In what ways did this leader demonstrate
Encourage the Heart?**

_____
....
_____
....
_____
....
_____

**How well did this leader exhibit the four
essentials?** What could the leader do to improve?

_____
....
_____
....
_____
....
_____

Expect
the best.

Personalize
recognition.

Create a spirit
of community.

Be personally
involved.

What were the benefits to the leader, the team, and individual team members for looking for ways to Encourage the Heart?

....

....

....

What can you apply in your own situation?

....

....

....

To Keep in Mind About Encourage the Heart

Leadership is more an affair of the heart than merely a matter of the mind.

There are virtually unlimited ways to show appreciation for accomplishments and to encourage perseverance.

Never underestimate the meaningful and lasting impact your genuine words of encouragement can have on others.

Work on your PNR—be generous with your positives.

Be authentic and real when you Encourage the Heart—make sure it's heart to heart.

Encourage the Heart Module Summary

The root word of the word "encourage" means heart. Leaders understand that in order to accomplish the extraordinary, people must have strong and committed hearts. When offering encouragement, the leader is in fact providing courage and strength to another person's heart.

To keep people inspired and willing to persevere on the long and challenging path to success, leaders:

- Make a point to constantly recognize excellence.

- Provide words of support and encouragement to express their belief and confidence in others.

- Show their appreciation for both the big and small things people do to achieve goals and model values.

Recognize contributions by showing appreciation for individual excellence.

Celebrate the values and victories by creating a spirit of community.

What are the three most important things you learned about the practice of Encourage the Heart?

1. ....

....

....

2. ....

....

....

3. ....

....

....

How will improving in the practice of Encourage the Heart help you address the leadership challenge that you brought to this workshop?

Think about these questions.

Which of your team members would really benefit from more recognition? How would you personalize it?

- -
. . . .
- -
. . . .
- -
. . . .
- -
. . . .

How frequently do you Encourage the Heart? What benefits to you and others would there be if you increased your PNR?

- -
. . . .
- -
. . . .
- -
. . . .

How personally involved are you with your team?

What is something you could do to show that you care? To perpetuate the stories? To be more involved in celebrations? To create a spirit of community?

Ideas into Action

• • • • • • • • • • • •

66 [Celebrations] are the punctuation marks that make sense of the passage of time; without them, there are no beginnings and endings. Life becomes an endless series of Wednesdays. 99

DAVID CAMPBELL,
SENIOR FELLOW WITH THE CENTER
FOR CREATIVE LEADERSHIP

• • • • • • • • • • • • • • •

"Leadership requires learning on the job. With the will power—and the heart—to continue, you can lead the way."

CHRISTIAN FUX,
INTERNATIONAL COMMITTEE OF THE RED CROSS, KENYA

COMMITTING

Committing

Every exceptional leader is an exceptional learner. Leadership development is an ongoing process that requires practice.

Many leadership skills can be learned successfully in the classroom, but we also learn from other people and from experiences. We must take advantage of every opportunity to practice our skills. We may fail, but we will learn from our mistakes.

MODULE OBJECTIVES

When you complete this module, you will be able to:

- Identify short-term and long-term actions for improving in one of The Five Practices

- Hold a conversation with your team and/or manager to share your LPI feedback, your values, and your vision of the future.

A Conversation About My Values and My Vision

MY VALUES

MY VISION

Worksheet: Identifying My Goals

1. **Review the notes you have made in this workbook and think about the insights you've had from the discussions and activities.** Then select ONE of The Five Practices on which you want to focus your leadership development during the next thirty days (short-term, immediate actions you can take right after the workshop) and over the next ninety days (longer-term actions that require some preparation).

Practice to focus on:

- -

A useful template for thinking about your goals follows:

"In [time period]**, I will** [improve, increase, decrease, or eliminate _____] **so that** [describe payoff for self and organization]. **My success will be measured by** [describe tangible or observable outcomes]."*

- -
. . . .
- -
. . . .
- -

*Reprinted from *The Six Disciplines of Breakthrough Learning* (p. 91) by C. Wick, R. Pollock, A. Jefferson, and R. Flanagan. Published by Pfeiffer, An Imprint of Wiley, 2006.

2. **Identify your short-term and long-term goals for improving the leadership practice you have chosen.** Think about why you selected the particular goals and decide what specific actions you will take to achieve them.

SHORT-TERM GOALS (WITHIN THIRTY DAYS):

GOAL

REASONS FOR SELECTING

ACTIONS FOR ACHIEVING

LONG-TERM GOALS (WITHIN NINETY DAYS):

GOAL

REASONS FOR SELECTING

ACTIONS FOR ACHIEVING

Which specific aspects of your challenge will be addressed by your meeting your goals?

- -

. . . .

- -

. . . .

- -

Which aspects of your challenge will require additional work?

How will achieving your goals help you meet your current leadership challenge?

- -

. . . .

- -

. . . .

- -

If you selected a challenge that was linked to specific team or organizational goals, how are the individual goals you've selected connected?
Will achieving your individual goals help the team or organization to achieve its goals?

- -

. . . .

- -

. . . .

- -

Worksheet: Planning a Conversation with Your Team and/or Manager

Use this worksheet to plan a conversation during which you will share with your team and/or your manager what you have learned about yourself as a leader and what actions you plan to take.

With whom will you have this conversation?

....

When and where will you have it?

....

....

What will you say to begin the conversation?

....

....

....

What key points will you cover?

....

....

....

How will you close the conversation?

....

....

....

What will you do to follow up on the conversation?

....

....

....

Sample Agenda

1. Welcome.

2. Why I asked you to be here.

3. What I learned about leadership and myself. (Values and lessons learned about my leadership abilities from the LPI feedback and the workshop.)

4. My thoughts about a shared vision and values for this team. (Project, program, community, organization.)

5. What I plan to accomplish. (My thirty- and ninety-day goals and the actions I'm going to take to achieve my goals.)

6. Your feedback on what I've been saying: What do you think about all of this?

7. Next steps. Some activities we can do around values, vision, and other suggestion you may have. (Setting up the next team meeting.)

8. "I appreciate your feedback and.... thank you."

Making Your Commitment

1. Do a "reality check" of your development plans: **Are they clear?** Do they make sense? Are there any additional ideas or suggestions that you might not have considered?

· ·

----

2. Make a promise to your colleague that you will take these actions.

3. Schedule at least two in-person or telephone meetings during which you will discuss what each of you did, what happened, what you learned, and what you will do next.

First meeting date and time (in about thirty days):

· ·

Second meeting date and time (in about ninety days):

· ·

Commitment partner's name

Telephone number:

E-mail address:

Commitment partner's signature:

Your Leadership Journey

We demonstrate our commitment to becoming a better leader—or to doing anything, for that matter—when we do three things:

- Freely choose actions.

- Go public with what we're going to do.

- Make it hard for ourselves to back out of our commitment to take those actions.

That's what you've done in this module. You have freely chosen goals you want to accomplish and actions you're going to take to achieve them. You made a public statement to at least one other person about what you're going to do. And you've made it harder to back out of your commitment by signing your commitment statement and arranging a time to talk about what you've done.

But the real test of your commitment comes when you leave *The Leadership Challenge® Workshop*. The true test is whether you "Do What You Say You Will Do" back in your organization. Your personal credibility will be strengthened the moment you take that first action step to apply what you've learned here.

We wish you continuing joy and success on your leadership journey!

JIM KOUZES

BARRY POSNER

What's Next?

Because effective leadership development is not an event but an ongoing process, we have designed a full range of resources to support leaders in continuing their development in The Five Practices following *The Leadership Challenge® Workshop*. These include:

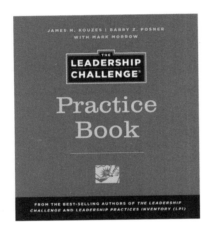

THE LEADERSHIP CHALLENGE PRACTICE BOOK

Helping leaders to actively use and improve their leadership skills in each of The Five Practices every day, the Practice Book guides leaders in daily activities to practice back on the job, and includes worksheets and grids for logging practice activities.

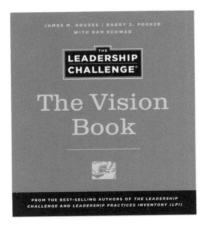

THE LEADERSHIP CHALLENGE VISION BOOK

This focused resource guides leaders through the process of developing and delivering their teams' vision messages and building their own and their teams' skills as visionaries.

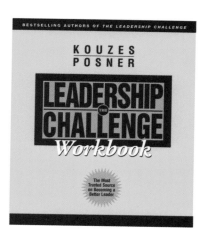

THE LEADERSHIP CHALLENGE WORKBOOK

This workbook is a hands-on guide for leaders to apply The Five Practices to a project of their choice, furthering their abilities to lead others to get extraordinary things done.

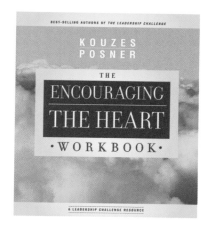

THE ENCOURAGE THE HEART WORKBOOK

For leaders seeking intense development in the fifth practice, Encourage the Heart, this self-study workbook provides detailed information and activities on mastering the four essentials of Encourage the Heart that will help them become more caring and credible leaders.

THE LPI LEADERSHIP DEVELOPMENT PLANNER

The planner picks up where the *LPI Participant's Workbook* leaves off and helps leaders review their progress and contains more than one hundred developmental activities for becoming a better leader.

APPENDIX

Answer Key

ORIENTEERING

page 7: Questions People Frequently Ask of Leaders

- Who are you?
- Where are we headed?
- What are you going to do?

CHALLENGE THE PROCESS

page 105: Helping People Take Risks and Learn from Mistakes

- Remember that to take risks, people have to feel safe.
- Set up a mechanism to keep people from hurting anyone if they fail.
- Build trust in the team.
- Reward people for sticking their necks out.
- Cheer people on.
- Send the message "You can do it!"
- Celebrate small wins.
- Discuss what worked/is working, what didn't/isn't, what needed/needs to be done differently, and how do better the next time.
- Be a role model

page 129: How to Give People More Control

- Share information

- Involve people in making decisions that affect their work and life.

- Allow discretion for decisions

- Back people up when they make a decision

- Assign non-routine jobs

- Clear away obstacles

- Eliminate non-essential rules

- Get people to talk about their goals, dreams, and plans for the future.

Suggestions for Becoming a Better Leader

MODEL THE WAY

- At the end of every day, ask yourself, "What have I done today that demonstrated one of my key values? What have I done today that might have sent the signal that I wasn't committed to that key value? What can I do tomorrow to live out a key value?"

- For every project you lead, set clear goals, make plans, and establish milestones.

- If you completed the Credo Memo activity, post your Credo Memo on the door to your office or the side of your cubicle where it will be visible to others. Invite people who stop by to read and have a conversation with you about it.

- If you completed the Credo Memo activity, revisit your Credo Memo in six months. Ask yourself if there are any values that you'd add, delete, or modify.

- Ask others on your team to write their credos and share them at one of your team meetings. Ask the team members to come to consensus about the values they're prepared to live out in their work. If you have a set of organizational values, compare your team's values to the organization's. If there's any incompatibility, resolve it.

- Do something dramatic to demonstrate your commitment to a team value. For instance, if creativity is a value, take everyone out to buy a few kids' games and spend a couple of hours playing them. Then spend an hour discussing what people learned about creativity that could be applied to their own work or to the organization.

- Every so often, trade places with one of your employees. It's a terrific way to get feedback on how others think you're doing (and to give feedback to someone else).

- DWYSYWD. Keep your daily organizer or calendar close at hand. Write down your promises as you make them and set a date for fulfilling them.

- Keep track of how you spend your time. Check to see whether your actions are consistent with your team's values. If you find inconsistency, figure out what you need to do to align your actions with the values.

- Develop a list of questions that you can ask to find out whether your team members are living out the team's values. Ask these questions at staff meetings. For example, ask people what they've done in the last week to make sure their work is top quality.

- Focus on the little things—not just the big ones—so that people know you value the quality of their work lives. Fixing a leaky roof is just as important as constructing a beautiful new building. What "leaky roofs" are there around your organization, and what can you do to fix them?

- Look for opportunities to talk with others about your values and beliefs. Put values on meeting agendas along with budget and schedules, and talk about values when planning projects.

- Make decisions visible. Use a centrally located bulletin board to post reminders of the team's decisions. Keep the board updated with information on progress.

- Be expressive (even emotional) about your beliefs. If you're proud of people for living up to high performance standards, let them know. Then brag about what they've done.

- Tell stories about people who are living out the values in memorable ways.

- Watch the film *Gandhi* with some colleagues. Afterward, discuss how Gandhi set an example for his constituents.

- Choose another famous leader you consider to be a role model. Learn whatever you can from that person by reading a biography or watching a film about him or her. Make notes about what you learn.

- Visit a retail store that's widely acknowledged for its extraordinary customer service. Watch and listen to what the store employees do and say. Shop there and see how you're treated. Interview a couple of the employees about how the store got such a stellar reputation.

- Read a book from the recommended list for Model the Way (see page 199).

INSPIRE A SHARED VISION

- Become a futurist. Join the World Futures Society. Read *American Demographics* or other magazines about future trends. Use the Internet to find a "futures" conference that you can attend. Make a list of what reputable people are predicting will happen in the next ten years.

- Every week, think of something you can do to clarify the kind of future you would like people to create together.

- Set up a process for looking ahead and forecasting future trends.

- Constantly look for ways in which you can get input from others on your vision, and encourage others to envision an uplifting and ennobling future.

- Keep a list of your constituents. Identify those you haven't reached out to yet and think about how you can learn more about their hopes and dreams.

- Set aside time at least once every month to talk about the future with your staff. Make your vision of the future part of a staff meeting, a working lunch, conversations by the water cooler, and so on.

- Read a biography of a visionary leader. Make notes about the way the person communicated vision and enlisted others in a common vision.

- Join Toastmasters or take a course in effective presentations to learn how to communicate your vision more effectively.

- Ask yourself, "Am I in the job to do something or am I in it for something to do?" Make a list of what you want to accomplish while you are in your current job—and why.

- Visualize what it will be like to attain your vision. Rehearse this scenario frequently in your mind.

- Read your vision speech to someone who will give you constructive feedback. Ask the person these questions: "Is the speech imaginative or conservative? Is it unique or ordinary? Does it evoke visual images? Is it oriented toward the future or toward the present? Does it offer a view that can be shared by others?"

- Hone your vision down to a short phrase of five to nine words that captures its essence.

- Regularly revisit and refine your vision. Think about events in the world, trends in your business, and changes in your life that might affect your vision.

- Look for CDs, tapes, podcasts, and videos of famous speeches by leaders who've inspired a shared vision. Learn everything you can from the masters. Keep a journal in which you note what you can use.

- Interview a speech writer. Ask him or her to share methods for constructing an inspirational speech.

- Read a book from the recommended list for Inspire a Shared Vision (see page 200).

CHALLENGE THE PROCESS

- At least once a month, set aside time to think about what challenging opportunities—new experiences, job assignments, tasks—you could seek to test your skills and abilities. Look for opportunities to ask for tough assignments.

- At least once a month, identify something you can do to challenge the way things are done—the status quo—at work. For example, think about what product or process innovations would help your organization improve. Then take the initiative to make change happen.

- Make a list of every task you perform. For each task, ask yourself, "Why am I doing this? Why am I doing it this way? Can this task be eliminated or done significantly better?"

- Examine every policy and procedure in your organization or unit. Ask "Why are we doing it this way?" If the answer is, "Because we always have," ask "How is it contributing to making us the best we can be?" If you can't come up with a satisfactory answer, eliminate or significantly improve the process or procedure so that it does contribute.

- Every few weeks, go shopping for ideas. Visit a local business—anything from a restaurant to a machine shop—with a colleague. Don't come back until you see one practice that a business does very well that your company could and should copy. Then do what you can to implement it.

- At least once a month, take a risk. Then take time to reflect on the results.

- When you make a mistake, ask, "What did I learn?" Discuss the mistake and what you learned with at least one other person.

- Regularly seek opportunities to encourage others to experiment, take risks, and learn from accompanying mistakes.

- When you begin a project, work with your team to break it into manageable chunks.

- Enroll in a class, course, or workshop dealing with a subject that you don't know anything about.

- Begin your next staff meeting with the following question: "What action did you take last week to make your performance even better this week?" Persist in asking this question for at least three meetings in a row so that everyone knows you're serious about continuous improvement. By the way, be prepared to answer this same question for yourself at each meeting.

- Hold a meeting with employees and ask them what really annoys them about the organization or unit. Commit to changing three of the most frequently mentioned items that are hindering success. Repeat this process every three months or so.

- Find something that's broken and fix it. Is it your calculator or your compensation system? Find something that isn't broken, but should be. Break it.

- Set up a pilot project for an innovative way of doing something—a new merchandising approach, a new intake process, a new procedure, new software that will make everyone more effective. Try it on a small scale first. Learn from it. Try some more.

- Reward risk-takers. Praise them. Give them prizes. Give them the opportunity to talk about their experience and share the lessons. It's money in the bank.

- Identify some successful people in your organization or other organizations who excel at challenging the process. Interview them about what they think are the ingredients for innovation and experimentation. Ask them how they "get away with" challenging the status quo.

- Read biographies about a couple of revolutionaries in business, science, politics, religion, or any endeavor. Learn whatever you can from the accounts of their lives. Note in your journal what you can use.

- Read a book from the recommended list for Challenge the Process (see page 200).

ENABLE OTHERS TO ACT

- Think about the ways in which projects are planned and decisions made in your organization. Then come up with several actions you can take to involve others in the planning and decision-making process.

- Think of several things you can do to develop cooperative relationships with people in your work group and with those in other parts of the organization.

- Hold a meeting in which the people on your team brainstorm ways in which you can treat others with real respect and create a climate in which people show respect for each other.

- Talk one-on-one with your team members to find out what kind of support and coaching they would like from you and what training opportunities they need. Find ways to connect people to the resources they need—other people, materials, funding, training, information, and so on.

- Increase opportunities for cross-functional or cross-organizational interaction. Establish common meeting areas that encourage people to interact. Bring a colleague from another area or team along to the next meeting. Schedule a lunch for two groups that don't spend much time face-to-face.

- List all your tasks, duties, and responsibilities. Identify those that you must do yourself and those that could be delegated to others. Then delegate—making sure that you provide those you delegate to with the necessary resources and support. Delegate the work and the responsibility.

- When a project lands on your desk, set up a planning meeting with all the people who will be involved.

- Commit to replacing the word "I" with "we" for at least the next two weeks. It's only a token of commitment to teamwork and sharing, but it will be noticed and valued.

- Never use the word "subordinate." Use "associate" or "team member."

- When something needs to be done, ask for volunteers. When you give people a choice about being a part of what's happening, they're much more likely to be committed.

- Assess the kinds of work that you have given people on your team to do. Does everyone have something to do that is important? If not, reassign some responsibilities. For example, arrange to have everyone in your group work with customers.

- Demonstrate respect and trust by regularly asking your co-workers for their opinions and viewpoints and sharing problems with them.

- When you make a mistake, admit it openly. When you don't know something, say, "I don't know." Show that you're willing to change your mind when someone comes up with a good idea.

- Enlarge people's sphere of influence. Make sure delegated tasks are relevant to the business. Increase people's ability to make decisions and remove unnecessary approval steps.

- Keep people informed. The more they know about what's going on in the organization, the more they will extend themselves to take responsibility and achieve extraordinary results.

- On a weekly basis, share information about how your unit is doing in terms of meeting its goals. People want to know how things are going. This information makes them feel more powerful.

- Substantially increase people's signature authority. When people are entrusted to spend the organization's money responsibly, they feel more in control of their own work lives.

- Volunteer to lead a professional, civic, or industry association. Working with volunteers will teach you collaborative skills and give you opportunities to use them.

- Hire a personal coach to help you improve in a specific leadership practice or a specific sport. Pay attention to this person's approaches and techniques and then try some of them with your own constituents.

- Choose someone in your organization who's known as an exceptional "people person." Accompany and observe this person interacting with others for a few hours. Ask for tips on how you can do better.

- Read a book from the recommended list for Enable Others to Act (see page 202).

ENCOURAGE THE HEART

- Think of ten little ways in which you can reward people who have done something especially well. Then reward those extraordinary efforts. Don't let them go by unnoticed or un-praised.

- Wander around your office area for the express purpose of finding someone in the act of doing something that exemplifies the organization's standards. Find a way to recognize that person on the spot.

- Identify bonuses and incentives you can use to encourage and reward people for exceptional performance.

- Ask yourself which of your constituents best embody your values and priorities. Think of three ways to single them out in the weeks to come, to praise and reward them.

- Describe three events or ceremonies you could use to give out individual awards.

- Create a "Hall of Fame" for individual contributors.

- Tell a public story about a person in your organization who went above and beyond the call of duty.

- Hold a team meeting in which you brainstorm ways of recognizing the achievements of others.

- Identify the next milestone your team is about to reach. What will you do to celebrate it?

- Think of three things you can do to Encourage the Heart in regularly scheduled meetings.

- Set aside one day a year for your team's Day of Celebration. Plan a special party or event for that day.

- Make heroes of other people. Publicize the work of team members. Shine the spotlight on at least one person each day. Who will you spotlight first?

- Think of innovative ways to recognize and reward people. For example, give a giant light bulb to the person who has the best idea of the month, or a chocolate kiss to a person who makes the office run "sweetly." Tailor ideas to your team.

- Say "thank you." Write at least ten thank-you notes and "You Made My Day" memos every week to praise people for jobs well done. If you can't find ten things to praise, look harder.

- Give people tools that they can use to recognize one another, such as index cards or notepads printed with the message "You Made My Day." Create a culture in which peers recognize peers.

- Provide feedback about results. Feedback is critical, and the sooner the better. Be specific. Instead of simply saying, "good work," describe what the person did and why it was "good work": "Your report was so complete and clearly written that I hardly needed to spend any time at all editing it." "We all appreciated the work you did to make the meeting run so smoothly."

- Be personally involved. Attend the staff parties and celebrations; otherwise, you'll send a message that you're not interested and don't consider them worth your time.

- Ask for advice and coaching from someone you know who's much better at encouraging the heart than you are.

- Talk to people in your organization who have a reputation for helping others to develop. Ask them how they encourage others to excel.

- Read a book from the recommended list for Encourage the Heart (see page 203).

- Be in love with what you are doing. Keep the magic alive.

Tips for Sharing Your LPI Feedback

Sharing your LPI feedback with your constituents—particularly those who provided the LPI–Observer data—offers an important opportunity to educate co-workers about the practices of leadership and to demonstrate your respect for their feedback and your commitment to the team.

With solid preparation, a feedback session will be valuable for you and your constituents. The fact that you are making the effort to share your LPI feedback will mean a lot to them.

GROUND RULES FOR FEEDBACK SESSION

Establishing some ground rules can help your feedback session go more smoothly and be more useful for both you and others.

- No personal attacks or reprisals.

- Focus on behaviors, not personalities.

- Connect behaviors with results or outcomes.

- No hearsay, accusations or exaggerations.

- Provide specific and constructive information.

- Include "positive" as well as "negative" feedback.

TIPS FOR RECEIVING FEEDBACK

- Make this a partnership process, not a debate.

- Focus energy on understanding, not fixing.

- Take feedback seriously. Bring a notepad and take notes.

- Ask questions ("Could you elaborate?"). Request specific examples. Confirm your understanding. ("If I understand correctly, you're saying...")

- Thank people for their feedback.

Further Reading to Support The Five Practices

GENERAL LEADERSHIP

Joseph Badaracco, *Defining Moments: When Managers Must Choose Between Right and Right*. Boston: Harvard Business School Press, 1997.

Warren Bennis, *On Becoming a Leader*. Reading, MA: Perseus, 1994.

James MacGregor Burns, *Leadership*. New York: HarperCollins, 1978.

Jim Collins, *Good to Great: Why Some Companies Make the Leap and Others Don't*. New York: HarperCollins, 2001.

Jim Collins, *Built to Last: Successful Habits of Visionary Companies*. New York: HarperBusiness, 1994.

Howard Gardner, *Leading Minds: An Anatomy of Leadership*. New York: Basic Books, 1995.

John Gardner, *On Leadership*. New York: The Free Press, 1990.

Bill George, *Authentic Leadership: Rediscovering the Secrets to Creating Lasting Value*. San Francisco: Jossey-Bass, 2004.

James M. Kouzes and Barry Z. Posner, *The Leadership Challenge* (4th ed.). San Francisco: Jossey-Bass, 2007.

James M. Kouzes and Barry Z. Posner, *The Truth About Leadership: The No-Fads, Heart-of-the Matter Facts You Should Know*. San Francisco: Jossey-Bass, 2010.

Tom Peters, *Liberation Management: Necessary Disorganization for the Nanosecond Nineties*. New York: Knopf, 1992.

Jeff Pfeffer and Robert Sutton, *Hard Facts, Dangerous Half-Truths and Total Nonsense: Profiting from Evidence-Based Management*. Boston: Harvard Business School Press, 2006.

Edgar H. Schein, *Organizational Culture and Leadership, second edition*. San Francisco: Jossey-Bass, 1992.

MODEL THE WAY

David M. Armstrong, *Managing by Storying Around: A New Method of Leadership*. New York: Doubleday, 1992.

James A. Autry, *The Servant Leader: How to Build a Creative Team, Develop Great Morale, and Improve Bottom-Line Performance*. New York: Three Rivers Press, 2004.

Warren Bennis, Daniel Goleman, and James O'Toole, *Transparency: How Leaders Create a Culture of Candor*. San Francisco: Jossey–Bass, 2008.

Po Bronson, *What Should I Do with My Life*? *The True Story of People Who Answered the Ultimate Question.* New York: Random House, 2001.

Steven R. Covey, *The Seven Habits of Highly Effective People*. New York: Simon & Schuster Inc., 1989.

Max De Pree, *Leadership Is an Art*. New York: Doubleday, 1989.

Alan Deutschman, *Walk the Talk: The #1 Rule for Real Leaders*. New York: Portfolio, 2009.

Bill George with Peter Sims, *True North: Discover Your Authentic Leadership*. San Francisco: Jossey-Bass, 2007.

Marshall Goldsmith, *What Got You Here Won't Get You There: How Successful People Become Even More Successful*. New York: Hyperion, 2007.

Marshall Goldsmith, *MOJO: How to Get It, How to Keep It, How to Get It Back If You Lose It*. New York: Hyperion, 2010.

Robert K. Greenleaf, *Servant Leadership: A Journey into Legitimate Power and Greatness*. New York: Paulist Press, 1983.

James M. Kouzes and Barry Z. Posner, *Credibility: How Leaders Gain and Lose It, Why People Demand It*. San Francisco: Jossey–Bass, 2003.

Ellen J. Langer, *Mindfulness*. Reading, MA.: Addison-Wesley, 1989.

David H. Maister, *Practice What You Preach: What Managers Must Do to Create a High Achievement Culture*. New York: The Free Press, 2001.

Parker J. Palmer, *Let Your Life Speak: Listening to the Voice of Vocation*. San Francisco: Jossey–Bass, 2000.

Terry Pearce, *Leading Out Loud: The Authentic Speaker, The Credible Leader*. San Francisco: Jossey–Bass, 1995.

Tony Simons, *The Integrity Dividend: Leading by the Power of Your Word*. San Francisco: Jossey–Bass, 2008.

Craig Wortmann, *What's Your Story? Using Stories to Ignite Performance and Be More Successful*. Chicago: Kaplan Publishing, 2006.

INSPIRE A SHARED VISION

Boyd Clarke and Ron Crossland, *The Leaders Voice: How Your Communication Can Inspire Action and Get Results!* New York: Select Books, 2002.

Edward Cornish, *Futuring: The Exploration of the Future*. Bethesda, MD: The World Future Society, 2005.

Belle Linda Halpren and Kathy Lubar, *Leadership Presence: Dramatic Techniques to Reach Out, Motivate, and Inspire*. New York: Gotham Books, 2003.

Gary Hamel, *Leading the Revolution*. Boston: Harvard Business School Press, 2000.

Chip Heath and Dan Heath, *Made to Stick: Why Some Ideas Survive and Others Die*. New York: Random House, 2007.

Jennifer James, *Thinking in the Future Tense: Leadership Skills for the New Age*. New York: Simon & Schuster, 1996.

Robert Johansen, *Leaders Make the Future: Ten New Leadership Skills for an Uncertain World*. San Francisco: Berrett-Koehler, 2009.

Robert Johansen, *Get There Early: Sensing the Future to Compete in the Present*. San Francisco: Berrett-Koehler, 2007.

James M. Kouzes and Barry Z. Posner, *A Leader's Legacy*. San Francisco: Jossey-Bass, 2006.

Richard Leider, *The Power of Purpose: Find Meaning, Live Longer, Better*. San Francisco: Berrett-Koehler, 2010.

John Naisbitt, *Mindset: Eleven Ways to Change the Way You See—and Create—the Future*. New York: HarperCollins, 2006.

Burt Nanus, *Visionary Leadership*. San Francisco: Jossey–Bass, 1992.

Daniel H. Pink, *Drive: The Surprising Truth about What Motivates Us*. New York: Riverhead Books, 2009.

Peter Schwartz, *The Art of the Long View*. New York: Currency, 1991.

Rajendra S. Sisodia, David B. Wolfe, and Jaqdish N. Sheth, *Firms of Endearment: How World-Class Companies Profit from Passion and Purpose*. Upper Saddle River, NJ: Wharton School Publishing, 2007.

Roy M. Spence, Jr., with Haley Rushing, *It's Not What You Sell, It's What You Stand For: Why Every Extraordinary Business Is Driven by Purpose*. New York: Portfolio, 2009.

Bruce Sterling, *Tomorrow Now: Envisioning the Next Fifty Years*. New York: Random House, 2003.

CHALLENGE THE PROCESS

Daniel Ariely, *Predictably Irrational: The Hidden Forces That Shape Our Decisions* (Revised and Expanded). New York: HarperCollins, 2009.

Arlene Blum, *Annapurna: A Woman's Place,* Twentieth Anniversary Edition. San Francisco: Sierra Club Books, 1998.

Mihaly Csikszentmihalyi, *Finding Flow: The Psychology of Engagement with Everyday Life*. New York: BasicBooks, 1997.

Richard Farson and Ralph Keyes, *Whoever Makes the Most Mistakes Wins: The Paradox of Innovation*. New York: The Free Press, 2002.

Richard Foster and Sarah Kaplan, *Creative Destruction: Why Companies That Are Built to Last Underperform the Market—and How to Successfully Transform Them*. New York: Currency, 2001.

Bill George, *Seven Lessons for Leading in Crisis. Value.* San Francisco: Jossey–Bass, 2009.

Malcolm Gladwell, *Blink: The Power of Thinking Without Thinking*. New York: Little, Brown, 2005.

Gary Hamel with Bill Breen, *The Future of Management*. Boston: Harvard Business School Press, 2007.

Ronald Heifitz and Marty Linsky, *Leadership on the Line: Staying Alive Through the Dangers of Leading*. Boston: Harvard Business School Press, 2002.

Rosabeth Moss Kanter, *Confidence: How Winning Streaks and Losing Streaks Begin and End*. New York: Three Rivers Press, 2007.

Tom Kelley with Jonathon Littman, *The Art of Innovation: Lessons in Creativity from IDEO, America's Leading Design Firm*. New York: Currency Doubleday, 2005.

Gary Klein, *Intuition at Work: Why Developing Your Gut Instincts Will Make You Better at What You Do*. New York: Currency Doubleday, 2003.

Robert J. Kriegel and Louis Patler, *If It Ain't Broke, Break It!* New York: Warner Books, 1991.

Salvatore Maddi and Deborah Khoshaba, *Resilience at Work: How to Succeed No Matter What Life Throws at You*. New York: AMACOM, 2005.

Randy Pausch with Jeffrey Zaslow, *The Last Lecture*. New York: Hyperion, 2008.

Michael Useem, *The Go Point: When It's Time to Decide—Knowing What to Do and When to Do It*. New York: Three Rivers Press, 2006.

ENABLE OTHERS TO ACT

Michael Abrashoff, *It's Your Ship: Management Techniques from the Best Damn Ship in the Navy*. New York: Warner, 2002.

Ken Blanchard, John Carlos, and Alan Randolph, *The Three Keys to Empowerment*. San Francisco: Berrett-Koehler, 1999.

Leigh Branham, *The Seven Hidden Reasons Employees Leave: How to Recognize the Subtle Signs and Act Before It's Too Late*. New York: AMACOM, 2005.

Hyler Bracey, *Building Trust: How to Get! How to Keep It!* Taylorsville, GA: HR Artworks, 2002.

Warren Bennis and Patricia Ward Biederman, *Organizing Genius: The Secrets of Creative Collaboration*. Reading, MA: Addison-Wesley, 1998.

Peter Block, *The Empowered Manager: Positive Political Skills at Work*. San Francisco: Jossey-Bass, 1987.

Marcus Buckingham and Curt Coffman, *First, Break All the Rules: What the World's Greatest Managers Do Differently*. New York: Simon & Schuster, 1999.

Cary Cherniss and Daniel Goleman, eds., *The Emotionally Intelligent Workplace: How to Select for, Measure, and Improve Emotional Intelligence in Individuals, Groups, and Organizations*. San Francisco: Jossey-Bass, 2001.

Robert B. Cialdini, *Influence: How and Why People Agree to Things*. New York: Marrow, 1984.

Steven M. R. Covey with Rebecca R. Merrill, *The Speed of Trust: The One Thing That Changes Everything*. New York: The Free Press, 2008.

Daniel Goleman, *Emotional Intelligence: Why It Can Matter More than IQ* (10th Anniversary Edition). New York: Bantam, 2006.

Daniel Goleman, Richard Boyatzis and Annie McKee, *Primal Leadership: Realizing the Power of Emotional Intelligence*. Boston: Harvard Business School Press, 2004.

Malcolm Gladwell, *The Tipping Point: How Little Things Make a Big Difference*. Boston: Little, Brown and Company, 2002.

Jon Katzenbach and Zia Kahn, *Leading Outside the Lines: How to Mobilize the Informal Organization, Energize Your Team, and Get Better Results*. San Francisco: Jossey-Bass, 2010.

Patrick Lencioni, *The Five Dysfunctions of a Team: A Field Guide for Leaders, Managers, and Facilitators*. San Francisco: Jossey-Bass, 2005.

Charlene Li, *Open Leadership: How Social Technology Can Transform the Way You Lead*. San Francisco: Jossey-Bass, 2010.

Kerry Patterson, Joseph Grenny, Ron McMillan, Al Switzler, *Crucial Conversations: Tools for Talking When Stakes Are High*. New York: McGraw-Hill, 2002.

Tom Rath, *Vital Friends: The People You Can't Afford to Live Without*. New York: Gallup Press, 2006.

Dennis Reina and Michelle Reina, *Trust and Betrayal in the Workplace: Building Effective Relationships in Your Organization*. San Francisco: Berrett-Koehler, 2006.

Dennis Reina and Michelle Reina, *Rebuilding Trust in the Workplace: Seven Steps to Renew Confidence, Commitment, and Energy*. San Francisco: Berrett-Koehler, 2010.

Evan Rosen, *The Culture of Collaboration: Maximizing Time, Talent, and Tools to Create Value in a Global Economy*. San Francisco: Red Ape Publishing, 2007.

Tim Sanders, *The Likeability Factor: How to Boost Your L-Factor and Achieve Your Life's Dreams*. New York: HarperCollins, 2006.

Pamela S. Shockley-Zalabak, Sherwyn Morreale, and Michael Hackman, *Building the High-Trust Organization: Strategies for Supporting Five Key Dimensions of Trust*. San Francisco: Jossey-Bass, 2010.

Jack Stack and Bo Burlingham, *A Stake in the Outcome: Building a Culture of Ownership for the Long-Term Success of Your Business*. New York: Currency Doubleday, 2002.

James Surowiecki, *The Wisdom of Crowds: Why the Many Are Smarter Than the Few and How Collective Wisdom Shapes Business, Economies, Societies and Nations*. New York: Anchor Books, 2005.

Kenneth W. Thomas, *Intrinsic Motivation: What Really Drives Employee Engagement* (2nd ed.). San Francisco: Berrett-Koehler, 2009.

ENCOURAGE THE HEART

Barbara L. Fredrickson, *Positivity: Groundbreaking Research Reveals How to Embrace the Hidden Strengths of Positive Emotions, Overcome Negativity, and Thrive*. New York: Crown Publishers, 2009.

Richard Boyatzis and Annie McKee, *Resonant Leadership*. Boston: Harvard Business School Press, 2005.

Nathen Branden, *The Six Pillars of Self-Esteem*. New York: Bantam Books, 1994.

Ken Blanchard and Sheldon Bowles, *Gung Ho! Turn on the People in Any Organization.* New York: William Morrow, 1997.

John Hope Bryant, *Love Leadership: The New Way to Lead in a Fear-Based World*. San Francisco: Jossey-Bass, 2009.

Terrence Deal and M. K. Deal, *Corporate Celebrations: Play, Purpose, and Profit at Work*. San Francisco: Berrett-Koehler, 1998.

Adrian Gostick and Scott Christopher, *The Levity Effect: Why It Pays to Lighten Up*. Hoboken, NJ: John Wiley & Sons, 2008.

Adrian Gostick and Chester Elton, *The Carrot Principle: How the Best Managers Use Recognition to Engage Their People, Retain Talent, and Accelerate Performance* (Updated and Expanded). New York: The Free Press, 2009.

Dave Hemsath and Leslie Yerkes, *301 Ways to Have Fun at Work*. San Francisco: Berrett-Koehler, 1997.

Alfie Kohn, *Punished by Rewards: The Trouble with Gold Stars, Incentive Plans, A's, Praise, and Other Bribes*. New York: Houghton Mifflin, 1999.

James M. Kouzes and Barry Z. Posner, *Encouraging the Heart: A Leader's Guide to Rewarding and Recognizing Others*. San Francisco: Jossey-Bass, 2003.

Ellen J. Langer, *Mindfulness*. Reading, MA: Addison–Wesley, 1989.

Bob Nelson, *1001 Ways to Reward Employees*. New York: Workman, 1994.

Tom Rath and Donald Clifton, *How Full Is Your Bucket: Positive Strategies for Work and Life.* New York: Gallup Press, 2004.

Leslie A. Yerkes, *Fun Works: Creating Places Where People Love to Work* (2nd ed.). San Francisco: Berrett-Koehler, 2007.

LEADERSHIP DEVELOPMENT

Ram Charan, S. Drotter, and J. Noel, *The Leadership Pipeline: How to Build the Leadership Powered Company*. San Francisco: Jossey–Bass, 2001.

Jay Conger and Rondal E. Riggio, eds. *The Practice of Leadership: Developing the Next Generation of Leaders*. San Francisco: Jossey-Bass, 2006.

Geoff Colvin, *Talent Is Overrated: What Really Separates World-Class Performers from Everybody Else*. New York: Portfolio, 2008.

Daniel Coyle, *The Talent Code: Greatness Isn't Born. It's Grown. Here's How*. New York: Bantam Books, 2009.

Carol S. Dweck, *Mindset: The New Psychology of Success*. New York: Random House, 2006.

K. Anders Ericsson, Neil Charness, Paul J. Feltovich, and Robert R. Hoffman, eds., *The Cambridge Handbook of Expertise and Expert Performance*. New York: Cambridge University Press, 2006.

Malcolm Gladwell, *Outliers: The Story of Success*. New York: Little Brown, 2008.

John P. Kotter and Dan S. Cohen, *The Heart of Change: Real-Life Stories of How People Change*. Boston: Harvard Business School Press, 2002.

Mary K. Schwartz, ed., *Leadership Resources: A Guide to Training and Development Tools* (8th edition). Greensboro, NC: Center for Creative Leadership, 2000.

Noel Tichy with Eli Cohen, *The Leadership Engine: How Winning Companies Build Leaders at Every Level*. New York: HarperCollins, 1997.

ABOUT THE AUTHORS

About the Authors

Jim Kouzes and Barry Posner are co-authors of the award-winning and best-selling book, *The Leadership Challenge*. This book was selected as one of the Top 10 books on leadership of all time (according to *The 100 Best Business Books of All Time*), won the James A. Hamilton Hospital Administrators' Book-of-the-Year Award and the Critics' Choice Award from the nation's book review editors, was a *BusinessWeek* best-seller, and has sold over 1.8 million copies in more than twenty languages.

Jim and Barry have co-authored more than a dozen other leadership books, including *A Leader's Legacy*—selected by *Soundview Executive Book Summaries* as one of the top thirty books of the year—*Credibility: How Leaders Gain It and Lose It, Why People Demand It*—chosen by *Industry Week* as one of its year's five best management books—*Encouraging the Heart*, *The Student Leadership Challenge*, and *The Academic Administrator's Guide to Exemplary Leadership*. They also developed the highly acclaimed *Leadership Practices Inventory* (LPI), a 360-degree questionnaire for assessing leadership behavior, which is one of the most widely used leadership assessment instruments in the world. More than four hundred doctoral dissertations and academic research projects have been based on the Five Practices of Exemplary Leadership® model.

Among the honors and awards that Jim and Barry have received are the American Society for Training and Development's (ASTD) highest award for their Distinguished Contribution to Workplace Learning and

Performance; Management/Leadership Educators of the Year by the International Management Council (this honor puts them in the company of Ken Blanchard, Stephen Covey, Peter Drucker, Edward Deming, Frances Hesselbein, Lee Iacocca, Rosabeth Moss Kanter, Norman Vincent Peale, and Tom Peters, who are all past recipients of the award); and named among the Top 50 Leadership Coaches in the nation (according to *Coaching for Leadership*).

Jim and Barry are frequent conference speakers, and each has conducted leadership development programs for hundreds of organizations, including Apple, Applied Materials, ARCO, AT&T, Australia Post, Bank of America, Bose, Charles Schwab, Cisco Systems, Community Leadership Association, Conference Board of Canada, Consumers Energy, Dell Computer, Deloitte Touche, Dorothy Wylie Nursing Leadership Institute, Egon Zehnder International, Federal Express, Gymboree, Hewlett-Packard, IBM, Jobs DR-Singapore, Johnson & Johnson, Kaiser Foundation Health Plans and Hospitals, L. L. Bean, Lawrence Livermore National Labs, Lucile Packard Children's Hospital, Merck, Mervyn's, Motorola, NetApp, Northrop Grumman, Roche Bioscience, Siemens, Standard Aero, Sun Microsystems, 3M, Toyota, the U.S. Postal Service, United Way, USAA, Verizon, VISA, and The Walt Disney Company.

JIM KOUZES

Jim Kouzes is the Dean's Executive Professor of Leadership, Leavey School of Business, at Santa Clara University. Not only is he a highly regarded leadership scholar and an experienced executive, but *The Wall Street Journal* has cited him as one of the twelve best executive educators in the United States.

In 2006 Jim was presented with the Golden Gavel, the highest honor awarded by Toastmasters International. Jim served as president, CEO, and chairman of the Tom Peters Company from 1988 through 1999, and prior to that led the Executive Development Center at Santa Clara University (1981–1987). Jim founded the Joint Center for Human Services Development at San Jose State University (1972–1980) and was on the staff of the School of Social Work, University of Texas. His career in training and development began in 1969 when he conducted seminars for Community Action Agency staff and volunteers in the war on poverty effort. Following graduation from Michigan State University (B.A. with honors in political science), he served as a Peace Corps volunteer (1967–1969). Jim also received a certificate from San Jose State University's School of Business for completion of the internship in organization development. Jim can be reached at **jim@kouzes.com**.

BARRY POSNER

Barry Posner is professor of leadership at Santa Clara University (Silicon Valley, California), where he has received numerous teaching and innovation awards and served as dean of the Leavey School of Business for twelve years (1996–2009). An internationally renowned scholar and educator, Barry is author or co-author of more than a hundred research and practitioner-focused articles.

He currently serves on the editorial review boards for *Leadership and Organizational Development*, *Leadership Review*, and *The International Journal of Servant-Leadership*. Barry is a warm and engaging conference speaker and dynamic workshop facilitator. Barry received his baccalaureate degree with honors from the University of California, Santa Barbara, in political science; his master's degree from The Ohio State University in public administration; and his doctoral degree from the University of Massachusetts, Amherst, in organizational behavior and administrative theory. Having consulted with a wide variety of public- and private-sector organizations around the globe, Barry currently sits on the board of director of EMQ Family First. He has served previously on the board of the American Institute of Architects (AIA), Junior Achievement of Silicon Valley and Monterey Bay, San Jose Repertory Theater, Public Allies, Big Brothers/Big Sisters of Santa Clara County, the Center for Excellence in Nonprofits, Sigma Phi Epsilon Fraternity, and several start-up companies. Barry can be reached at **bposner@scu.edu**.

Aftercare